I0007616

Bubble.io Made Easy

A STEP-BY-STEP GUIDE FOR NO CODE BEGINNERS AND INTERMEDIATE USERS

NEW EDITION! UPDATED ON APRIL 2025

By Daniel Melehi

Contents

Introduction

Welcome to *Bubble.io Made Easy: A Step-By-Step Guide for No Code Beginners and Intermediate Users*. I'm excited to take you on this journey of exploring everything Bubble has to offer. In this book, we'll unravel each layer of Bubble's no-code ecosystem, from creating simple applications to more complex platforms, all without writing a single line of code. If you're intrigued by the possibility of turning your ideas into functional web apps in record time, you're in exactly the right place.

I remember the days when just the thought of building an application seemed overwhelming. The technical jargon, the endless lines of code, and the constant worry of not knowing enough to get started felt like roadblocks. That's precisely why I put together this guide: to provide a confident, friendly voice that leads you through every core concept and capability that Bubble has to offer. I'll share practical tips, examples, and insights I've gathered while building my own apps using Bubble.

WHY BUBBLE IS A GAME-CHANGER

In my experience, Bubble stands out because it helps people focus on what truly matters—solving problems—without getting tangled in complex code. With its visual editor, fast prototyping capabilities, and robust integration options, Bubble encourages creativity and experimentation for makers at every level. Whether you're a complete novice or have dabbled in no-code environments before, you'll find Bubble's approach both accessible and versatile.

WHO THIS BOOK HELPS

This guide is built with first-time users in mind, but it also caters to those who have some experience in Bubble yet want a deeper understanding of advanced features. By the time we're done, my goal is for you to feel comfortable tackling a wide range of projects—be it a simple to-do list app, a marketplace, or something entirely original you've dreamt up.

WHAT TO EXPECT

As we progress, we'll cover everything from setting up a free Bubble account to fine-tuning your app's database structure, creating workflows, integrating payments, and even diving into advanced topics like scheduling backend workflows. By the end of the book, you'll not only have a stronger foundation for building apps with Bubble but also the confidence to push your creativity further.

MY PROMISE TO YOU

I've organized the chapters in a way that highlights the most important topics first, before progressively introducing more challenging concepts. At each stage, you'll find examples, checklists, and step-by-step instructions aimed at making sure you can follow along without feeling lost. I'm a firm believer that no idea is too complicated or too small to be built in Bubble, and I can't wait to see what you create.

Let this be your starting point on a journey to becoming a confident no-code developer. Now, let's begin exploring Bubble together, one step at a time!

Chapter 1: Understanding No-Code Development

When I first stumbled upon the idea of creating applications without traditional coding, I was immediately intrigued. I remember thinking how it felt almost magical to drag and drop elements on a screen and see my app take shape before my eyes. This is the essence of no-code development: it removes the barriers of needing extensive programming skills and lets you transform your ideas into fully functional apps. Throughout this chapter, I'll share my insights on the rise of no-code platforms, what makes Bubble particularly powerful, and how you, as a beginner, can benefit from this revolutionary approach.

EMBRACING THE NO-CODE MINDSET

One thing I learned quickly is that using a no-code platform like Bubble isn't just a matter of learning new tools—it's also about adopting a new outlook on problem-solving. In traditional development, you might spend hours wrestling with syntax, debugging code, or wrestling with complex servers. With no-code, your main challenge shifts to clearly defining what you want the application to do. Instead of thinking about complex programming languages, you think about workflows, data structures, and user experiences. It's a refreshing perspective that opens doors for people with different backgrounds—whether you're an entrepreneur, a designer, or just someone with a great idea.

THE EVOLUTION OF SOFTWARE DEVELOPMENT

Before no-code platforms emerged, building even a modest web application required a deep understanding of programming languages, frameworks, and databases. The introduction of Visual Basic decades ago was an early sign that drag-and-drop development was possible, but widespread adoption truly took off in recent years with far more advanced toolkits and online platforms. As businesses began demanding faster prototypes, agile methodologies, and cost-efficient solutions, no-code solutions came to the forefront. They accelerated the development process while reducing the steep learning curve once associated with software creation.

WHAT MAKES BUBBLE STAND OUT

There are plenty of no-code and low-code platforms out there, but Bubble has a unique edge. Its drag-and-drop interface is more than just a simple layout tool: it's a canvas for designing dynamic, data-driven experiences. Here's why I think Bubble shines:

- **All-in-one environment:** Bubble offers design, database, and workflow functionality within a single platform, so you don't have to piece together multiple services.
- **Extensive plugin ecosystem:** Any time you need extra capabilities—like integrating with third-party APIs or adding specialized design elements— you'll likely find a plugin ready to go.
- **Scalability:** You can start small and grow as your user base expands, all without transitioning to another platform later on.
- **Flexibility:** Whether you're building a basic to-do list or a complex marketplace, Bubble's capabilities adapt to your unique requirements.

CORE PRINCIPLES OF NO-CODE

While no-code development can feel different from traditional approaches, it's built on a few fundamental principles:

Simplicity: By abstracting away the code, no-code platforms let you focus on the essential features and user experience. Think of it like designing with building blocks rather than mixing raw building materials.

Rapid Prototyping: Because you can visually design and immediately test your app, it's easier to iterate, gather feedback, and refine. This cuts down development time dramatically.

Logic through Workflows: No-code platforms replace pages of code with logic-based steps. You'll define "when this happens, do that" sequences that connect your inputs, data, and final outputs.

Focus on User Experience: Since developers aren't bogged down by syntax, there's much more room to invest time in perfecting the app's look and feel, which often translates to better products overall.

DEBUNKING MYTHS AND MISCONCEPTIONS

I've met people who believe no-code means "no complexity" or that only small-scale prototypes are possible. In fact, no-code can handle a broad range of projects—including fully featured web applications. There's also a misconception that no-code eliminates the need to learn anything technical. Many no-code tools, Bubble included, require an understanding of workflows and data structures. However, that learning curve is typically far gentler than picking up a full-stack programming language.

REAL-WORLD USE CASES

I've seen no-code solutions used everywhere from small nonprofits looking to organize event registrations, to entrepreneurs launching e-commerce platforms, and even established businesses creating internal dashboards. With Bubble, you can build:

- **Marketplaces:** Allow users to buy, sell, and exchange goods or services.
- **Social Networks:** Bring communities together around shared interests.
- **Project Management Tools:** Organize tasks, track progress, and collaborate in real time.
- **Internal Dashboards:** Summarize company data and metrics in an easily digestible format.

KEY ADVANTAGES FOR BEGINNERS

As someone who's guided newcomers through the no-code process, I can't emphasize enough how empowering it can be to see your ideas come to life quickly. Here are some key benefits for those just starting out:

1. **Accessibility:** You don't need to be a developer by trade or have a formal computer science background to build fully functioning apps.
2. **Cost Savings:** Hiring a development team can be expensive, especially for early-stage projects. A no-code approach helps you validate ideas without a massive budget.
3. **Creative Freedom:** By providing a suite of design and logic tools, Bubble encourages you to experiment, test new features quickly, and pivot if needed.
4. **Fast Learning Curve:** While there's still some learning involved, it's often faster to master workflows and visual design than to learn a new programming language from scratch.

PREPARING FOR THE JOURNEY AHEAD

As we embark on this journey together, I encourage you to keep an open mind. Embracing no-code might initially feel like stepping into uncharted territory—especially if you're used to more traditional methods or if you've never built an app before. But the potential here is enormous, and once you get comfortable with Bubble's workspace, you'll have a new set of creative possibilities at your fingertips.

In the chapters that follow, we'll explore how to set up your Bubble account, navigate the editor, establish a database, and craft essential workflows. We'll also look at ways to integrate external services and make your app both appealing and responsive. By understanding the core ideas behind no-code development, you're already one step closer to building the solutions you've been dreaming up.

Now that we've set the stage on what no-code is and why it's a powerful approach, let's roll up our sleeves and dive into making your Bubble journey a reality.

Chapter 2: Setting Up Your Bubble.io Account

CREATING YOUR BUBBLE.IO PROFILE

When I first signed up for Bubble, the registration process was straightforward. You simply head to the Bubble.io website, click "Sign Up," and enter your email and password—no fuss, no complicated steps. After creating my credentials, I received a confirmation email to verify my account, which was quick and easy. Once I confirmed, I was officially part of the Bubble community and ready to start exploring. It felt exciting to realize how accessible full-scale app development could be, all just by setting up this account.

CHOOSING A PLAN THAT FITS

One of the aspects that drew me to Bubble was their range of pricing plans. The Free plan is generous enough to let you explore and build prototypes without worrying about elevated costs. However, if you plan on launching a commercial project or need premium features, you can upgrade to a paid plan at any time. When I was ready to take my prototypes public, I switched to a plan that provided more database capacity and removed Bubble's branding. My advice is to start small with the Free plan, especially when you're exploring and learning. This approach keeps things simple and lets you grow at your own pace.

SECURING YOUR ACCOUNT

Security was a big priority for me, and fortunately Bubble offers two-factor authentication, email verification, and other measures that protect your account. After signing up, I navigated to my Settings page to enable two-factor authentication. This extra step adds another layer of security by requiring a special code from my phone each time I log in. I find it comforting to know that even if someone obtained my password, they'd still need that unique code.

EXPLORING THE DASHBOARD

The Bubble Dashboard is where you'll manage your apps, link external domains, and review logs. When I first landed on the Dashboard, I spotted a button labeled "New App"— the gateway to creating my very first project. The dashboard also keeps track of your plan details, usage limits, and any plugins you've installed. If you're like me and love staying organized, you'll appreciate how neatly everything is laid out for easy access.

STARTING A NEW PROJECT

To kick off my first app, I clicked on "New App" and gave my project a name. While it might be tempting to jump right into building, taking a moment to plan your app's purpose and functionality can save time later on. Once the project was created, Bubble offered the option to start with a blank canvas or choose a pre-built template. I chose a blank one to better acquaint myself with the Editor's features. If you prefer a head start, templates can be a fantastic way to learn by example.

INVITING TEAM MEMBERS

Even as a solo creator, I've found the collaboration tools in Bubble incredibly helpful. You can invite team members to your application from the Settings panel in the Dashboard. Granting people varying levels of access—like read-only or full editor rights—ensures that everyone can contribute effectively without stepping on each other's toes. When I collaborated with a friend on a project, we appreciated how Bubble made version control straightforward and kept track of each revision we made.

MANAGING PROJECT SETTINGS

Once the app is set up, there are several important settings to configure. By clicking on the "Settings" tab in the Editor, you can upload a logo for your application, set a custom domain (if you have one), and define email addresses for automated messages. This is also where you'll establish SEO settings if you want your app to be discovered via online searches. I've learned the hard way that filling in these details early on can prevent headaches down the road, especially if you plan on going live soon.

STAYING ORGANIZED FROM THE START

A small but meaningful tip I picked up was to keep my Bubble workspace organized from day one. Naming my apps clearly, labeling pages according to their functionality, and using consistent naming for data types and workflows helped me avoid confusion later. It's a habit I developed once I realized how quickly a project can grow in complexity. By being tidy with how I label elements and data structures, I could easily find things later, even after months away from a project.

NEXT STEPS ON YOUR JOURNEY

After you've set up your account and have a new app ready, you're closer than ever to bringing your ideas to life. Leave any intimidation behind—the real magic here is in the building. In the upcoming chapters, I'll share how to navigate the Editor in depth, connect your app securely to its database, and craft all sorts of custom workflows. The simple act of setting up a Bubble account is the foundation on which you'll be building interactive, engaging applications. Take a moment to appreciate how far you've already come, and get ready to dive into the fun of visually constructing your app's unique features.

With that, your Bubble account is fully operational, and you're equipped to start exploring. Tournament brackets, booking platforms, internal dashboards—whatever your vision might be, this is where it all begins. As you move forward, keep experimenting, stay curious, and remember that every new app starts with this simple yet powerful setup process.

Chapter 3: Navigating the Bubble Editor

FAMILIARIZING YOURSELF WITH THE EDITOR LAYOUT

When I first opened the Bubble Editor, I was immediately drawn to its clean, intuitive design. At the heart of this workspace is a large canvas where I can see my app pages come to life. To the left, I spotted a sidebar with tabs labeled "Design," "Workflow," "Data," "Styles," "Plugins," and more. Each tab has a specific purpose, and mastering how they work together has made building apps feel like second nature. The top bar includes controls for previewing my app, accessing version history, and checking logs, while the right side offers a dynamic panel that changes based on the elements or workflows I'm editing.

THE DESIGN TAB: YOUR CREATIVE PLAYGROUND

The "Design" tab is where I spend the bulk of my time visually constructing each page. I can drag and drop elements—like text, buttons, inputs, and even entire repeating groups—straight onto the canvas. What initially surprised me was how flexible these elements can be. For instance, if I drop a button, I can easily resize it, change its color, or link it to a workflow, all without a single line of code. I also noticed a sidebar within the Design tab that organizes all the available elements into categories like "Visual Elements," "Input Forms," and "Containers." Having these groups keeps me from feeling overwhelmed when I'm looking for a particular component.

WORKFLOW TAB: CRAFTING APP LOGIC

Next on the left sidebar is the "Workflow" tab, where I fine-tune an app's logic. Whenever a user clicks a button or loads a page, I can define step-by-step instructions for how the app should respond. In my experience, this tab is where the magic truly happens. I can pick from a variety of actions—like creating a new data entry, sending an email, or displaying an alert—and chain them together in a visual format. At first, it felt a bit like learning a new language, but I appreciated how each step was described in plain English. The more I experimented, the more I realized that nearly everything I wanted to automate could be accomplished here.

DATA TAB: BUILDING A STRONG APP BACKBONE

Without a structured database, an application's functionality can unravel quickly. The "Data" tab lets me design the app's data types, fields, and privacy settings. It's where I define how the app stores information and who can access it. For example, if I'm creating an event-planning app, I might set up a "Event" data type with fields like "Date," "Location," and "Attendees." This tab also shows me all my app data in a spreadsheet-like view, which helps me debug and keep tabs on what users are submitting. One thing that really helped me was the ability to import and export data, which I found useful for both backups and rapid testing.

STYLES TAB: CONSISTENT DESIGN AT SCALE

Early in my Bubble journey, I noticed that creating consistent design guidelines was crucial for a professional look. The "Styles" tab made it easy to define uniform styles for buttons, text headings, input fields, and more. Whenever I change a style—say, updating the font size or color—it automatically applies to every element that uses it across the app. This saved me huge chunks of time when I wanted to give my entire application a fresh, cohesive appearance. I see it almost like having a master style sheet that keeps my design tidy and consistent.

PLUGINS TAB: EXTENDING YOUR APP'S CAPABILITIES

Bubble's impressive plugin ecosystem is another reason I quickly fell in love with the platform. By opening the "Plugins" tab, I discovered a library of third-party integrations for payment processing, social media logins, advanced charting, and beyond. Installing a plugin is typically as simple as clicking "Install," and then configuring it based on the instructions provided. I like to think of plugins as mini toolboxes that instantly expand my app's potential without having to code those features from scratch. The best part is, if I ever decide a plugin isn't right for my project, I can remove it with a single click, keeping everything clean and organized.

SETTINGS & VERSIONS: FINE-TUNING AND MANAGING UPDATES

The "Settings" area in the Bubble Editor houses a range of options, from SEO configurations to domain mapping and language preferences. Whenever I'm gearing up to launch, I often double-check these settings to ensure everything is aligned—like connecting a custom domain and adjusting performance settings. There's also a section for "Versions," which allows me to create and manage branches of my app. This version control system protects against accidental mistakes and lets me experiment with new features in a safe environment. You can merge changes, roll back updates, or collaborate with others without fear of messing up the live app.

NAVIGATING THE RIGHT PANEL: PROPERTIES AND REFERENCE

On the right side of the Editor, there's a dynamic properties panel that changes depending on what I've selected in the canvas. If I click on a button, I'll see its layout, style, and conditional options. If I click on a workflow event, I'll see all the possible actions and transitions. This context-based approach keeps me from having to dig through endless menus. I also love the built-in reference checker, which notifies me if an element or action is no longer valid. It's like having a personal assistant that gently taps me on the shoulder whenever something needs my attention.

PREVIEW AND DEBUG MODE: TESTING YOUR BUILD

When I'm ready to see how my app looks to an actual user, I hit the "Preview" button in the top bar. Bubble opens a new tab where I can experience my app just like a visitor would. I often toggle "Debug mode" to test how workflows run behind the scenes, step by step. This feature has been invaluable for diagnosing issues—like finding out which workflow step is slowing down a page or confirming whether a condition is being recognized correctly. I treat this preview mode as a safe space to refine everything before revealing the app to the world.

TIPS FOR EFFICIENT NAVIGATION

- **Use Search:** At the bottom of the Elements Tree, there's a search bar that helps me quickly locate any element on the page, saving time on large projects.
- **Shortcuts:** Bubble supports keyboard shortcuts like Ctrl/Cmd + Z for undo or Ctrl/Cmd + Y for redo. They're small tricks that can vastly speed up my workflow.
- **Tabs and Workspaces:** Don't be afraid to have multiple tabs open for the same app—one on the "Design" tab and another on "Data," for example. Jumping between them can help you tackle tasks more efficiently.
- **Responsive View:** Although there's a separate responsiveness feature, checking how your design adapts at smaller screen sizes early on can prevent layout problems down the road.

SEEING THE BIG PICTURE

When I first approached the Bubble Editor, it felt like entering an art studio full of tools I'd never used before. Over time, I realized every feature is there to empower my creativity, from the visual components to the data structures and workflows that make my app interactive. Keeping an eye on all these elements in unison—rather than managing them in isolation—helped me build intuitive interfaces that users genuinely enjoy.

What's been truly transformative is how the Editor's layout nudges me to think like a product designer and developer at the same time. While I'm tweaking a button style, I'm reminded of the underlying data or workflows. Conversely, while writing a workflow, I might notice a design flaw and jump to fix it. This seamless interplay is what sets Bubble apart for me, making every project both efficient and fun to build.

In the following chapters, I'll delve deeper into specialized features of the Editor, along with tips on database organization, workflows, and advanced functionality. But for now, getting comfortable navigating the Editor is a major milestone. By mastering these core tabs and panels, you're on a fast track to building fully functional, visually appealing apps. Take your time experimenting, and soon enough, the Bubble Editor will feel like second nature.

Chapter 4: Pages, Elements, and Layout Fundamentals

UNDERSTANDING THE ROLE OF PAGES

When I first started building apps in Bubble, I noticed how each "page" serves as a distinct environment for different functionalities—much like individual chapters within a book. Pages hold the structure, design, and user interactions that make up your entire application. For example, you might have a "Home" page that greets new visitors, a "Dashboard" page for logged-in users, and a "Profile" page for personal details. Organizing content this way helps keep everything tidy and makes navigating between sections more intuitive.

One thing I learned early on was to plan my page layout before dragging any elements onto the canvas. By asking myself, "Which aspects of my app need their own dedicated screen?" I could avoid clutter down the road. While some creators prefer using one page and multiple hidden groups (like a single-page application), dividing your app into separate pages remains a great choice when you want clear boundaries for user flow or improved performance.

CREATING AND MANAGING MULTIPLE PAGES

To add a new page, I simply click the "New page" option in the page dropdown at the top of the Bubble Editor. Naming the page is important—keeping names descriptive ("Dashboard," "Profile," or "Settings") helps you stay organized. Once you've set up multiple pages, you can navigate between them in the editor by selecting the page name from that same dropdown. I rarely find myself overwhelmed, thanks to the easy-to-use interface.

If you ever need to copy an existing page—maybe you like a particular layout and want to reuse it—Bubble lets you clone pages to jump-start your workflow. Once cloned, you can adjust the design or rename data fields, preserving the core structure as needed. This ability to duplicate pages has saved me countless hours when creating pages that share a similar style or functionality.

ESSENTIAL ELEMENTS FOR BUILDING YOUR APP

In Bubble, everything you see on a page—from text labels and images to input fields and buttons—is considered an **element**. Once I understood how each element interacts with the underlying workflows, app creation became much easier. Elements fall into various categories:

- **Visual Elements:** Text, shapes, images, icons— anything that contributes to how your app looks.
- **Input Forms:** Fields, dropdowns, and checkboxes that gather user data.
- **Containers:** Groups, repeating groups, and other structural components that help organize content.
- **Reusable Elements:** Components like headers or footers that can be used across multiple pages for consistency.

I remember feeling like a kid in a candy store the first time I scrolled through all the elements. While it's fun to mix and match, it's also wise to be strategic about what you add. Each element should serve a clear purpose—does it display information, gather input, or enhance navigation? Keeping this in mind prevents visual clutter and improves the user experience.

STRUCTURING YOUR LAYOUT WITH CONTAINERS

In my own designs, I like to rely on **groups** and **columns** to anchor the layout. Groups are wonderful for bundling multiple elements together and applying shared design settings. For instance, I might create a group containing a title, a short description, and a call-to-action button. Applying padding, background colors, or rounded corners to that group ensures a consistent look.

I also discovered that **repeating groups** are essential when displaying a list of data, like a set of product names or upcoming events. By setting a repeating group's data source, each cell automatically populates with items from the database—no need to manually replicate elements. It's a terrific way to keep your app dynamic and maintain a tidy interface.

LEVERAGING BUBBLE'S LAYOUT ENGINE

Bubble's layout engine has evolved to offer more responsive and flexible design options. Whether you choose a **fixed width** page or make it **full-width**, you can easily tailor the design to fit your desired user experience. One approach I find helpful is using horizontal and vertical alignment to ensure elements scale properly on different devices. This helps maintain a visually balanced layout, even when viewed on mobile screens.

You can also opt for the **new responsive engine**, which uses "rows" and "columns" to organize elements in a grid-like structure. I've found that setting the minimum and maximum widths, as well as potential breakpoints, helps control how my design adjusts on various screen sizes. Although it might feel a bit complex initially, spending time tweaking these settings can significantly enhance your app's overall look and feel.

ELEMENT POSITIONING AND ALIGNMENT

When I first started placing elements on the page, I sometimes struggled with positioning. It's tempting to place everything randomly, but Bubble provides alignment tools that snap elements into place. Grids and guide lines appear as you move elements around, which helped me ensure consistent spacing. There's also a handy option to center elements horizontally or vertically within a group. These small features might sound minor, yet they make a big difference in how professional your pages appear.

When designing complex pages, I often break them down into stacked groups. For instance, a heading group at the top, a main content area in the middle, and a footer group at the bottom. This modular approach not only keeps the editor organized but also makes it simpler to move or resize whole sections if I need to make broader design changes later.

COMBINING ELEMENTS FOR INTERACTIVITY

A good layout doesn't just look good—it feels intuitive to use. Buttons, icons, and clickable text must stand out enough to signal interactivity. To guide my users effectively, I sometimes add hover effects or subtle animations. For instance, letting buttons darken slightly when hovered over can hint at their clickable nature.

I also pay attention to element states—particularly with input fields. By highlighting an active input field (for example, changing its border color) or showing an error message if data is invalid, I can make the app more user-friendly. A well-designed layout is one that helps users navigate each step without confusion.

COMMON LAYOUT MISTAKES TO AVOID

Overcrowding: Filling every inch of space with elements can overwhelm users. It's better to keep some white space for breathing room.
Misusing Groups: Forgetting to group related elements makes it harder to reposition or adjust them later. Grouping is your friend—use it!
Lack of Hierarchy: Everything can't be made equally important. Headlines, buttons, and body text should have distinct sizes to guide users through your content.

Ignoring Alignment: Unguided alignment can make your interface look amateur. Use Bubble's alignment cues to keep things neat and consistent.

PRACTICAL LAYOUT STRATEGIES

When I'm mapping out a new page, I sometimes start with a rough sketch on paper. This helps me outline where the header goes, how the content is divided, and what the user's journey should look like. Then, I replicate that layout in the Bubble Editor. By staying true to my initial plan, I make fewer design tweaks mid-build. Of course, experimentation can still spark creative ideas, but having a basic blueprint keeps me grounded.

Additionally, I periodically preview my work on different devices—on desktops, tablets, and phones—to see if the layout holds up. If something appears off, it's often because I need to adjust margins or switch up the arrangement of elements into columns or rows. Immediately catching these issues ensures a more polished final product.

PUTTING IT ALL TOGETHER

Pages, elements, and layout choices form the backbone of any Bubble application. Once you understand how they fit together, designing and iterating becomes much more intuitive. Think of it as setting the stage for a performance: the page is your theater, elements are your actors, and the layout is the script that tells them where to stand and what to do. The more deliberate you are in each choice, the smoother your app will feel to users.

With the right mix of well-structured pages, thoughtfully placed items, and a clean, responsive layout, you can transform any idea into a user-friendly, visually appealing Bubble application. With these basics under your belt, you'll be better prepared to incorporate more advanced features into your design—like custom states or integrated APIs—without getting lost in messy page organization.

By mastering these layout fundamentals, you're setting the stage for a more efficient build process and a polished end product. In upcoming chapters, we'll dive deeper into workflows and data, but keep in mind that a solid layout is the frame on which all those other pieces rely. As you move forward, take the time to experiment, play around with grouping and responsive settings, and refine your layout until it clicks. Trust me, the effort will pay off in an app that's both functional and inviting.

Chapter 5: Adding and Configuring Workflows

BRINGING YOUR APP TO LIFE

When I first realized how powerful Bubble workflows could be, it felt like I was unlocking the engine under the hood of my application. While visual design shapes what the user sees, workflows determine what happens when they interact. Whether it's saving data to the database, navigating to another page, or triggering an email, each action relies on well-crafted workflows. With just a few clicks, I could design complex sequences that would normally require lines of code. This chapter offers an in-depth look at how I approach adding, configuring, and refining workflows, so your own app gains a dynamic, interactive quality.

IDENTIFYING WORKFLOW TRIGGERS

Whenever I plan a workflow, I start by identifying its trigger—what event or condition sets it in motion. Bubble provides a variety of trigger options that cover both user actions and automated processes. Some of my favorites include:

- **Element-Based Triggers:** Clicking a button, submitting a form, or hovering over an icon can all initiate a workflow.
- **Page Events:** Workflows can also be triggered when a page is loaded or when the user scrolls to a specific area.
- **Custom Events:** These user-defined triggers run when you call them in another workflow—handy for repeating a set of actions in multiple places.
- **Conditionals:** "Do when condition is true" triggers let you specify exactly when you want something to happen, such as displaying a warning message if a user's cart is empty.

Determining the right trigger is key to ensuring your workflow fires at the best possible time. For instance, a "Button Click" trigger makes sense if you want to log in a user only after they tap "Sign In." Meanwhile, a "Do when condition is true" trigger might be more useful for real-time checks in the background. By mapping out these scenarios in advance, I avoid confusion and keep my workflows well-organized.

DESIGNING THE ACTION SEQUENCE

Once I've nailed the trigger, I move on to defining the action or series of actions. In Bubble, actions are like building blocks that can be stacked to create the functional flow a user follows. You can do things like:

- **Create, Modify, or Delete Data:** Manage records stored in your app's database, such as adding a new user profile or updating an existing entry.
- **Send Emails or Text Messages:** Send notifications, confirmations, or alerts right away, or schedule them for a later time.
- **Navigate to a Different Page:** Route users to a success screen, dashboard, or external URL once they've completed an action.
- **Display Alerts:** Small pop-up messages are perfect for providing immediate feedback about what just happened—like "Your message has been sent!"

Each action in a workflow can either be conditionally triggered or always triggered. I often rely on conditionals to refine the logic. If I'm sending a welcome email to new users, for instance, I might add a condition to ensure it only goes out once—on their very first sign-in. Fine-tuning actions like this keeps my app experience both relevant and efficient.

USING STEP-BY-STEP LOGIC

A key advantage Bubble offers is the ability to chain multiple actions in a single workflow, one after another. Let's say I'm building a job board application. When a job is posted, I might:

1. **Create a Job Listing:** Store it in the database with fields like title, company, and location.
2. **Send a Confirmation Email:** Notify the poster that their job is live.
3. **Trigger Analytics Event:** Track the posting action to gather insights on user engagement.

All these steps happen in a tidy sequence, which keeps me from juggling separate workflows for a single user action. Beyond simplicity, chaining actions also improves maintainability: if I need to update the process later, I can edit it in one place rather than multiple.

WORKFLOW CONDITIONS AND DYNAMIC DATA

I love how Bubble lets me weave dynamic data into my workflow steps. If my workflow sends an email, I can personalize the subject line with the user's name. If my workflow creates a unique profile, I can generate a custom URL. Each time I reference dynamic data, I use expressions that pull real-time values from the user's input or the database. This is helpful when:

- **Auto-Filling Fields:** Prefill user details in a signup form or pre-select a shipping address in a checkout flow.
- **Filtering Queries:** Limit search results to items that match the user's preferences.
- **Triggering Calculations:** Calculate discounts or taxes based on user-entered figures.

Conditions often go hand in hand with dynamic data. If a user's account level is "Premium," I might give them extra workflow steps—like showing exclusive content or applying a loyalty discount. This level of customization allows me to tailor the experience for different segments of my user base without building separate apps.

SCHEDULING AND RECURRING WORKFLOWS

Sometimes, I need a workflow that runs at a specific time or repeats periodically—like sending out weekly newsletters or generating end-of-month reports. Bubble provides a feature to schedule these workflows in the future or set them as recurring events. For example, I've used scheduled workflows to:

- **Generate Weekly Metrics:** Summarize user activities, then email myself a report every Monday morning.
- **Issue Reminders:** Send a gentle nudge to users whose subscriptions are about to expire within 48 hours.

While setting these up, Bubble lets me choose the date and time as well as the data to pass into the workflow. It essentially takes care of the "when" and "what," so I only have to design the logic once. However, I make sure to keep track of potential user inactivity or old data because scheduled workflows will still fire, even if a user never revisits the site. A quick check is always wise to confirm that each scheduled event is still valid.

WORKFLOW RELIABILITY AND ERROR HANDLING

In my experience, carefully managing error conditions is just as important as building the main flow. Bubble includes features that help you confirm whether each step completed successfully. If something fails—like a payment processing action or an API call—Bubble can generate an error message or log the issue so I can diagnose it. I often add fallback steps to handle unexpected scenarios. For instance, if a user tries to register with an invalid email format, I can stop the workflow and display an appropriate error. This ensures the app feels robust and guides users to resolve mistakes right away.

TEST-DRIVING WORKFLOWS

One of my personal rules is to test workflows meticulously. It's easy to assume everything fits together, only to discover a missing condition or a misspelled field name when a user tries it for the first time. To avoid these pitfalls, I often:

Test Phase	Activities
Preliminary	Run through each workflow step in the Bubble Editor, checking for obvious errors in expressions or data bindings.
Live App Check	Switch to the live or preview mode and replicate different user actions—like signup, login, or form submission.
Edge Cases	Test unusual user inputs (invalid emails, extreme text lengths) to confirm your error handling is on point.

By following a structured testing approach, I catch potential issues early. Plus, I can keep an eye on the Debugger to see if each action is firing correctly. This sort of iterative test-fix-test cycle makes my workflows more reliable and my app more trustworthy.

BEST PRACTICES FOR ORGANIZED WORKFLOWS

One of the pitfalls I've found is letting my workflow logic sprawl out of control. It happened to me when I built a large marketplace app with a dozen different user flows—things got jumbled quickly. To stay organized:

1. **Label Everything Clearly:** Add descriptive names or notes for each workflow so you remember its purpose at a glance.
2. **Use Custom Events:** For actions repeated across multiple pages, define a custom event and call it whenever necessary. This cuts down on duplicating logic.
3. **Modularize Large Workflows:** If one workflow features too many steps, consider splitting it into smaller ones linked by conditions or custom events.

Adopting these practices keeps the Bubble Editor clean, making it easier to revisit or scale up your project. It's much simpler to add new features or debug issues when each workflow has a focused purpose, rather than cramming everything into a monolithic process.

PRACTICAL USE CASE EXAMPLE

Let me share a quick, real-world example. Suppose I'm building a membership site offering premium courses. When a user upgrades their membership, I need to:

- **Charge Their Payment Method:** Process the transaction using a payment integration or plugin.
- **Grant Elevated Permissions:** Update their user role in the database to "Premium," which unlocks restricted content.
- **Send a Welcome Message:** Personalize an email or in-app alert confirming their new benefits.

- **Log an Analytics Event:** Track the upgrade in a third-party analytics tool to measure conversion rates.

All four actions belong in a single, cohesive workflow triggered by the "Upgrade" button. By ensuring the payment is successful before I modify the database or send confirmations, I can handle partial or failed payments gracefully. It's a straightforward yet multi-step flow—a perfect example of how workflows can orchestrate pivotal actions behind the scenes.

EMBRACING CONTINUAL REFINEMENT

I've learned that workflows aren't a "set it and forget it" component. User feedback, new features, and changing requirements inevitably require adjustments. Thankfully, Bubble's visual approach makes it less daunting to open an existing workflow, insert a new step, or alter a condition. Over time, my apps evolve to become more efficient and user-friendly, and these iterative improvements often happen right inside the workflow editor.

Ultimately, well-planned workflows make all the difference in how smoothly an application functions. By taking the time to choose the right triggers, chain actions effectively, and stay organized, I can confidently build robust processes that respond to users in real time. Whether you're automating a simple form submission or orchestrating a complex series of events, workflows are what elevate your

Bubble creation from static pages to an interactive experience.

Chapter 6: Database Structure and Data Types

When I first began exploring Bubble's database features, I remember feeling both excited by the possibilities and a bit overwhelmed. In traditional coding environments, database set-up typically involves writing queries, configuring tables, and wrestling with obscure commands. Bubble, on the other hand, brings a visual approach that allowed me to build robust data structures without diving into complicated syntax. In this chapter, I'll share the ins and outs of how I approach defining data types, setting up fields, and organizing relationships—so that you can keep your app's information neat, secure, and easy to manage.

WHY DATABASE STRUCTURE MATTERS

Before we jump into the how-to portion, let's talk about the "why." Any application that handles user information, content, or transactions needs a solid underlying structure. A well-planned database ensures that data can be created, retrieved, and updated smoothly. In my experience, a poor structure often leads to sluggish performance, confusing user experiences, and difficulties in scaling your app. Conversely, a coherent database design can save countless hours of refactoring down the road, making your application more maintainable and efficient.

DEFINING DATA TYPES

In Bubble, a "data type" is essentially the foundation for any group of information you want to store—things like "User," "Event," or "Product." The goal is to clearly define the properties (fields) that each instance of this data type will have. For instance, a "User" data type might include fields for a person's name, email address, and profile picture.

When creating a new data type, I find it helpful to keep the name singular (e.g., "Event" rather than "Events"). This helps me stay consistent when referencing specific database entries later on. I also spend a moment brainstorming all the pieces of information that might become relevant. Even if I don't fill every field initially, having them defined up front keeps my database organized as the app evolves.

CHOOSING THE RIGHT FIELD TYPES

After you've set up a data type, the next step is choosing the proper field types. In Bubble, you have several options, such as "text," "number," "date," and "yes/no," as well as file and image fields. Each one is designed for specific use cases:

- **Text:** Stores any letters, numbers, or symbols (like user bios, titles, or descriptions).

- **Number:** Perfect for prices, scores, or any numeric value you might want to calculate or compare.
- **Date:** Useful for events, deadlines, or timestamps. Bubble can easily handle date comparisons and scheduling.
- **Yes/No:** Also known as booleans, which are basically "true" or "false" values. Ideal for toggling features or indicating status fields.
- **File/Image:** Lets you store user-uploaded items like photos, PDFs, or other documents.

While naming these fields, I like to keep the titles simple and self-explanatory. For example, if a data type is "Task," then the field "Due Date" is clear, whereas something like "DD" might be confusing to late-night me or future collaborators.

SINGLE ENTRIES VS. LISTS OF ENTRIES

One of the more powerful aspects of Bubble's database is the ability to store references to other data types, or even lists of them. A field can hold a single item, such as "Preferred Writer," referencing one "User" data type entry. Or, it can hold a list of many items, like "Attendees" for an event, referencing multiple "User" entries at once. This is particularly helpful for building relationships.

If I'm working on a team project app, for example, I might have a data type called "Project" that includes a field "Team Members," which is a list of the "User" data type. Each project can reference a handful of users, and each user can link to multiple projects in return (if I also add a field on the user side). This "lists" feature satisfies a variety of scenarios, whether you're associating products with categories or users with forum posts.

OPTION SETS VS. DATA TYPES

Bubble also includes a feature called "Option Sets," which is handy for fixed lists of values—like states, countries, or membership levels. While a data type might be more suitable for dynamic data, an option set helps control a predefined list, ensuring consistency throughout your app. For instance, if you have membership levels like "Basic," "Pro," and "Premium," an option set can lock down these choices and make them easy to reference across different pages and workflows. I like to think of them as controlled vocabularies that reduce the risk of typos, which might otherwise lead to messy results in your database.

STRUCTURING ONE-TO-ONE AND ONE-TO-MANY RELATIONSHIPS

When designing your database, consider how each data type interacts with others. Here are two common relationships you'll often encounter:

- **One-to-One:** Use a reference field on one data type that points to exactly one instance of another data type. This might be something like a "User" linking to a single "ProfileDetails" data type if you prefer to store extended information in a separate place.

- **One-to-Many:** Use a list field to reference multiple instances. For example, a "Recipe" data type could have a field "Ingredients," which is a list of the "Ingredient" data type. That allows you to easily loop through each ingredient when displaying the recipe details on the front end.

Defining these relationships carefully ensures that retrieving connected data in your workflows becomes an easy process, rather than a tangle of conditionals and manual searches.

EFFICIENT NAMING CONVENTIONS

Early on, I overlooked naming conventions, and it turned into a headache once my app had dozens of data types and fields. Now, I make sure to create clear, readable field names. If you have a data type called "Customer," fields might read "firstName," "lastName," "emailAddress," and "phoneNumber." This might seem trivial, but it's a lifesaver when searching through workflows or debugging issues.

WORKING WITH DATA PRIVACY

Data privacy is crucial if your app handles sensitive information. Bubble includes privacy roles that can be configured to restrict who sees or edits certain data. By going into your data settings, you can specify rules like "Only the user who created this thing can view and modify it" or "Admins can see all fields." I've found that setting these rules early in my project helps avoid accidental exposure of private details. You can always refine them as your app grows, but having a baseline data privacy structure in place is a healthy practice to adopt at the start.

PLANNING FOR SCALABILITY

One of the questions I get often is whether Bubble's database can handle large-scale applications. In my experience, it certainly can, as long as you design your data types and relationships thoughtfully. Here are a few tips I've picked up:

1. **Keep Data Types Lean:** Resist the urge to store rarely used details in the main data type.
   Sometimes it's better to create a separate data type or use option sets for seldom-changed properties.
2. **Avoid Overusing Lists:** While lists are convenient, a massive list can slow down queries. For extremely large datasets, consider a more segmented approach or set up additional linking data types.
3. **Index Key Fields:** By default, Bubble keeps things efficient, but naming key fields consistently and structuring relationships in a logical manner makes data retrieval smoother.

DEBUGGING AND REFINEMENT

If something ever feels off—like data not showing up or failing to save—Bubble's logs and the debug panel are invaluable. I'll typically preview the app, trigger a workflow, and watch the debugging tool highlight which data is being read or written. This step-by-step view helps pinpoint issues like a missing field or a mismatched data type. Whenever I spot a pattern of errors, I take it as a cue to revisit my data structure or privacy settings. Sometimes a small tweak—such as allowing a user role to view certain fields—can make all the difference in a seamless user experience.

BRINGING IT ALL TOGETHER

Crafting a healthy database in Bubble boils down to planning. Giving each data type a distinct purpose, choosing sensible field types, and defining relationships carefully set you up for success. Whether you're building a content-driven blog, an ecommerce marketplace, or a sophisticated booking platform, your database plays the silent but essential role of storing and delivering information behind the scenes.

My advice is to step back and think about how your real-world entities relate to each other before clicking the "Create new data type" button. Once you've mapped that out, Bubble's visual tools make it straightforward to bring these relationships to life. The more thoughtfully you structure your data from the start, the easier it becomes to create intuitive workflows, generate meaningful analytics, and scale your app to handle thousands—or even millions—of records.

So, whether you're new to database design or simply new to Bubble's approach, I hope this primer clarifies how everything fits together. By giving each data type the care and attention it deserves, you're laying the foundation for a successful application that meets user needs seamlessly. There's real satisfaction in watching your database flourish alongside your growing app, and I can't wait for you to experience that journey first-hand.

Chapter 7: User Authentication and Security Basics

One of the first questions I asked myself when building an application with Bubble was, "How do I protect my users' data and make sure only the right people can access certain features?" The good news is that Bubble has a built-in system for user authentication and security settings that can help keep your app's information safe. In this chapter, I'll walk you through how to leverage these tools effectively, from setting up sign-up and login flows to configuring advanced security rules. By understanding these fundamentals, you'll feel more confident about safeguarding both your users' privacy and your own peace of mind.

BUBBLE'S BUILT-IN USER SYSTEM

Bubble automatically provides a **User** data type, which is unique among your database structures because it stores key information like email addresses and passwords. This data type underpins your entire authentication system. Whenever someone creates an account in your app—whether by entering basic details like email and password or by logging in via a social service—the data is stored under this **User** record.

For me, the convenience starts there: I don't need to manually hash passwords or handle complex sign-up tokens. Bubble covers all the fundamental security aspects behind the scenes, making it less likely for user data to be improperly exposed. And if you want to add custom fields to your **User** type (such as display name, profile picture, or membership level), you can easily do so in the "Data" tab, just like you would with any other data type.

SETTING UP THE SIGN-UP WORKFLOW

When I first learned Bubble, I was excited by how effortless it was to create a sign-up flow. Generally, I'd place an input element for "Email" and "Password" on a page and then add a button labeled something like "Create Account." From there, the real magic happens in the workflow:

- **Event Trigger:** The user clicks the "Create Account" button.
- **Action:** Select "Account > Sign the user up."
- **Parameters:** Specify which input fields hold the email and password.

At this point, Bubble takes over. It creates the new User entry in the database, encrypts the password, and logs the user into the app—all in one neat process. If something goes wrong—like a missing password—it'll display an error message by default, or you can add your own custom alert for a more personalized user experience.

DESIGNING A USER-FRIENDLY LOGIN

Logins in Bubble follow a similar path. Commonly, I place a "Log In" button on a header or a dedicated login page. Once clicked, a workflow action labeled "Log the user in" prompts for the email and password fields. If the login is successful, Bubble seamlessly transitions the user to a protected or dashboard page; if not, you can display an error. For a professional touch, I sometimes create a "Remember Me" checkbox, which uses *Custom States* or additional logic to keep the user logged in beyond a single session.

Additionally, you can incorporate a "Forgot Password?" link to reset credentials. Bubble provides a built-in action to send password reset emails, removing the need for complicated third-party integrations. This simple addition can really streamline your user experience and boost overall security, since it encourages users to keep their account details updated without hassle.

SOCIAL MEDIA SIGN-ON

If you want to let users log in via Google, Facebook, or other social platforms, Bubble supports **OAuth2** integrations through plugins. After installing the relevant plugin from the "Plugins" tab, you'll typically configure your app's credentials in that provider's developer console. For instance, if you're enabling Google sign-in, you'll register your Bubble app with Google, then paste in your Client ID and Client Secret.

Once everything is set, adding a social sign-in button is relatively straightforward. Your workflows will include an action like "Sign in with Google" or "Sign in with Facebook," and Bubble automatically handles the token exchange in the background. The resulting user record in the database may pull basic info like their name or profile photo, further simplifying onboarding.

PROTECTING PAGES AND DATA

Once a user is logged in, not every page should be fair game. In my apps, I might reserve certain pages (like "Admin Dashboard") for users with specific roles or let only registered members access premium content. Bubble's **page-level security** can be managed by adding a rule that checks *"Only when Current User is logged in"* before allowing access, or in more advanced cases, verifying the user's role stored in a custom field. If the condition fails, I redirect them to a "Not Authorized" page. This simple guardrail helps ensure sensitive pages aren't openly accessible.

Beyond pages, you can tighten security within the **Data Privacy** panel, defining which fields a non-logged-in or basic user can see, versus someone with admin privileges. This is a more granular way to control access and can be crucial if you handle confidential info—like financial details or personally identifiable data. I like to think of it as a set of gates ensuring each user only sees what they're meant to see, no matter how clever they are at guessing URLs or hacking around the UI.

TWO-FACTOR AUTHENTICATION (2FA)

For improved account protection, you might consider enabling **2FA**, a mechanism that requires users to present a secondary authentication method—usually a one-time code sent to their phone or email. Bubble doesn't natively include 2FA for user logins, but you can implement it using plugins or external services like *Authy* or *Google Authenticator* APIs. Here's the general idea:

1. **Generate a Code:** When a user attempts to log in, your app requests a temporary code from the 2FA provider.

2. **Send Code:** A text or email (or an authenticator app) delivers the code to the user's device.
3. **Verification:** The user enters the code, and Bubble verifies it with the provider. If correct, they're granted full access.

While this adds a step to the login flow, it significantly enhances security. I've found it particularly helpful in apps where sensitive data or financial transactions require added protection, giving users peace of mind that their accounts won't be compromised by simple password guessing.

SECURING WORKFLOWS

Beyond gatekeeping who can see what, you'll also want to ensure that only authorized actions can occur within your app. For instance, if a user modifies a "Project" data record, do they have the right permission level for that operation? In Bubble, you can enforce checks right inside your workflows. For instance, a workflow titled "Delete Project" might include a condition: *"Only when Current User's Admin? is 'yes'"* or *"Only when Project's Creator is Current User".* If the condition isn't met, the action simply doesn't fire.

It's easy to overlook these details when first designing your app. I recommend methodically reviewing each workflow step to confirm that no unauthorized user can manipulate data or escalate privileges. The more advanced your app's complexity, the more crucial it is to keep these security measures front and center.

HANDLING SENSITIVE DATA

If your application deals with highly sensitive information—think medical records, banking data, or confidential legal documents—you'll need extra care. Bubble already encrypts passwords by default but consider these extra steps:

- **Limit Access via Privacy Roles:** Assign strictly who can view or edit each field. You can base these rules on whether the record's creator is the current user, or if the user has a specific role.
- **Obfuscate or Mask Data:** Hide or partially obscure fields in your UI so only necessary details are visible. This can be done using conditional formatting, like showing only the last four digits of a social security number or credit card.
- **Utilize External Encryption Services:** If needed, you can integrate external encryption tools before storing data in Bubble's database. This approach can add even more layers of protection for certain fields.

MONITORING LOGS AND USER ACTIVITY

Keeping an eye on who's doing what in your app helps detect suspicious behavior and maintain overall health. Bubble provides basic **logs** that list errors, workflow events, and user sign-ups. By reviewing them periodically, you can spot unusual spikes in login attempts or repeated errors that indicate someone might be probing for vulnerabilities.

When I manage multi-user apps, I often create an admin-only dashboard that displays recent sign-ins, new user registrations, and error spikes. This lets me respond more quickly if accounts appear compromised or if workflows are failing more often than usual. Simple monitoring goes a long way in catching issues before they escalate into full-blown threats.

PROTECTING YOUR OWN BUBBLE ACCOUNT

As the app creator, it's your responsibility to secure your Bubble account itself. After all, if someone gains access to your Bubble Editor, they could view database records, modify code, or lock you out entirely. I strongly recommend:

- **Enabling Two-Factor Authentication:** Bubble allows 2FA for your own login, making it tougher for outsiders to hijack your development account.
- **Using Strong, Unique Passwords:** Avoid reusing passwords from other services to minimize risk if one of your other accounts is compromised.
- **Managing Team Permissions:** Grant only the necessary level of access to collaborators. For instance, a read-only role for testers who don't need to make editor changes.

Taking these steps ensures that the keys to your entire application are protected, preserving not only your own work but also the safety of your users' data.

COMMON PITFALLS AND HOW TO AVOID THEM

Over time, I've seen a few recurring mistakes when it comes to security in Bubble apps. Here are some you'll want to dodge:

Pitfall	Avoidance Strategy
Blanket Permissions	Don't give every user access to all data by default. Think carefully about who needs to view or edit each record.
Weak Passwords	Implement minimum password lengths or complexity checks, encouraging users to choose stronger credentials.
Unrestricted Admin Roles	Limit how many admin accounts exist, and regularly review which email addresses you've designated as admins.
Hardcoding Sensitive Data	Never store API keys or other secrets in plain text. Use Bubble's built-in

secret management or environment
variables when possible.

REFINING YOUR SECURITY OVER TIME

Developing an app is never a static process, and your
security measures shouldn't be either. As your user base and
feature set grow, new threats or vulnerabilities can surface.
I like to schedule periodic security reviews—at least
quarterly—to revisit privacy rules, check for admin
accounts that aren't needed anymore, and monitor any third-
party changes, such as updated OAuth policies.

Each time I add a new functionality—like messaging
between users or file uploads—I think through the potential
risks. Who can see these messages? What file types are
allowed? Setting up workflows and privacy roles properly
from the get-go counters issues before they evolve into
security holes. This ongoing attention ensures that your app
doesn't just look good and run smoothly, but also stands up
to real-world security demands.

By now, it should be clear that Bubble's user authentication
system and security settings are potent tools, but they still
rely on you to put them to use with intention and savvy.
With a little planning and strategic thinking, you can forge
a protected environment that fosters user trust—and that's
one of the key ingredients to any successful app.

Chapter 8: Connecting External APIs

One of the most exciting moments I've experienced in my Bubble journey was realizing just how easily I could extend my app's capabilities by integrating external APIs. Suddenly, the world of third-party services—ranging from social media platforms to payment gateways—opened up, and I no longer had to implement everything from scratch. In this chapter, I'll share the ins and outs of connecting external APIs in Bubble, focusing on what you need to know to get your app talking seamlessly with outside services. By the end, you'll be ready to pull data from nearly any source, update information on the fly, and even automate some of your app's core processes.

WHY EXTERNAL APIS MATTER

Before we dive into the technical details, let's clarify why external APIs are such a game-changer. APIs, or **Application Programming Interfaces**, let separate systems communicate and exchange data. When you use Bubble's visual interface to interact with an external API, you effectively bridge your app with a world of specialized services. Here are a few examples I've found particularly handy:

- **Social Media Integrations:** Display recent tweets or post automatically on Instagram.
- **Payment Processing:** Send transaction details to PayPal, Stripe, or other merchant services.

- **Location** & **Maps:** Convert addresses to coordinates, show customizable maps, and fetch real-time traffic updates.
- **Analytics** & **Reporting:** Push data to external dashboards or retrieve metrics for business insight.

By leveraging these capabilities, you can reduce the workload on your app, enrich user experiences with real-time information, and even coordinate tasks that would otherwise require separate tools—and all of it without touching raw code.

ENABLING THE API CONNECTOR

Bubble's main gateway to the outside world is the **API Connector plugin**. Accessing it is straightforward. First, head over to the "Plugins" tab in the Bubble Editor. If you haven't already, click "Add plugins" and search for "API Connector." Once you've installed it, a new configuration menu appears, giving you the power to define and manage external services.

When I first explored the API Connector, I was pleasantly surprised by the clarity of its interface. Fields like "API name," "Authentication," and "Body Type" guide you through the setup. Even if the terminology seems unfamiliar at first, each step is structured enough that I quickly got the hang of it—and I'm confident you will, too.

BASIC SETUP: DEFINING CALLS

In Bubble, each **API Call** describes a specific request you want to make. Whether you're retrieving data (GET), sending new data (POST), updating entries (PATCH/PUT), or deleting items (DELETE), you'll create a call that outlines these details. Here's how I typically do it:

1. **Give it a Name:** I pick something descriptive, like "Fetch Current Weather" or "Create New Invoice."
2. **Choose the Method:** Select GET, POST, PUT, or DELETE based on what the external service's documentation instructs.
3. **Enter the URL Endpoint:** Paste the service's endpoint URL. For instance, a weather service might look like
   https://api.weather.org/current?location=....
4. **Headers and Params:** If the API needs special headers (like "Content-Type: application/json") or query parameters, I add them here. This is also where you'd jam in credentials if the API uses API keys or tokens.

Once the call is defined, I can run a quick test right from within the API Connector to confirm if the response data looks right. Seeing that JSON response appear in real time gave me a huge sense of accomplishment the first time I tried it.

UNDERSTANDING AUTHENTICATION OPTIONS

APIs often want proof that your app is allowed to request their data. This proof is called **authentication**. Bubble's API Connector supports various methods, so let's take a quick look at the most common ones:

- **API Key in URL/Header:** Some services simply require a key appended to your request. For instance, *?api_key=your-key.* You can store that key in the connector so it's added automatically on each call.
- **Bearer Token:** More secure APIs typically need an *Authorization: Bearer <token>* header. After retrieving the token once (sometimes via username and password), you place it in each call's header. Think of it like a keycard you need to show for every door.
- **OAuth2:** If you want a user to log in via a service like Google, Slack, or HubSpot, you'll often go through an OAuth2 "handshake." Bubble's integrated approach simplifies token retrieval and refreshes, so you don't have to handle that manually.

The best way to figure out which method to use is to check the documentation of the external service. Once you know the method, Bubble's interface guides you through the necessary steps. I've also found it helpful to keep credentials in environment variables or in Bubble's secure fields, ensuring I don't accidentally expose them in public areas of my app.

DISPLAYING DATA IN YOUR BUBBLE APP

Pulling data from an external source is only half the battle; you also need a slick way to present it. Bubble excels here, thanks to dynamic expressions. Once I designate my repeating group's data source as the external API call, each row or cell can automatically populate with the JSON fields returned by the API.

For instance, say I'm showing weather info. I can create a repeating group that references the "Fetch Current Weather" call, and each cell might show a different city's temperature and condition. With a little styling, it looks just like a native Bubble data display—but behind the scenes, everything is powered by that external feed. In the same fashion, a single group or text field can show data if I'm only returning one object.

SENDING DATA AND ACTIONS

While reading data is common, you'll often want to **send information** to an external API, too. I've done this for tasks like posting new records to a CRM or scheduling a meeting in Google Calendar. In these cases, I configure the call as POST or PUT and specify the *JSON body* or *form data* the API expects. This might look something like:

{ "title": "New Event", "start_time": "2023-12-01T10:00:00", "end_time": "2023-12-01T11:00:00" }

In the API Connector, I'll map each field to a dynamic value from Bubble—for example, a form input that collects the event title. Then, whenever my user clicks "Schedule Event," that data zips off to the external service, creating the record on their end. If a response comes back confirming success, I can display a success message or update the UI accordingly. It's a potent way to orchestrate multi-tool workflows without writing any raw code.

HANDLING ERRORS AND DEBUGGING

I'd be lying if I said external API calls always worked perfectly the first time. Sometimes you get incorrect JSON formatting, or you realize you left out a required parameter. Luckily, Bubble helps with **debugging** efforts in several ways:

- **API Connector "Initialize Call" Feature:** After defining a call, you can "Initialize" it to see if the response structure is valid. If there's a problem, Bubble typically shows an error message to guide you.
- **Browser Console and Logs:** If something fails during a user-triggered workflow, I'll open the app's built-in logs or the browser console to catch the exact error text or status code.
- **Postman or Similar Tools:** On particularly confusing setups, I'll use a separate tool like Postman to confirm the call works outside Bubble. Once I'm sure the external service is acting as documented, I'll replicate the same headers and body in Bubble's connector.

Although debugging can feel tedious, each step teaches me something new about how the API works. By staying patient and making small, incremental changes, I quickly adapt to each service's quirks.

TIPS FOR EFFICIENT API CONNECTIONS

Over time, I've picked up a few best practices that keep my API integrations clean and scalable:

Tip	Why It Helps
Use Reusable Calls	Instead of creating multiple calls for similar tasks, define a single call with dynamic parameters so you maintain just one source of truth.
Secure Your Keys	Store API keys in Bubble's hidden fields or environment variables. Exposing keys publicly can lead to unauthorized usage.
Cache Data Locally	If the external data doesn't change often, consider saving it in your Bubble database to reduce repeated external calls.

Stay Within Rate Limits	Most APIs limit how frequently you can call them. Plan your workflows to avoid hitting service-imposed throttles.

SCHEDULING API WORKFLOWS

Sometimes you don't need immediate data from an external service, but rather periodic updates. For instance, I once built a website that fetched currency exchange rates daily. Bubble's **backend workflows** let me schedule a recurring event that automatically calls the API every 24 hours, storing fresh rates in the database. This freed my front-end from constantly making requests, and users always saw the latest rates without any noticeable delay. By combining external APIs with scheduled tasks, you can automate routines like sending newsletters, syncing databases, or updating product inventories—well beyond what you'd typically associate with a no-code platform.

KEEPING SECURITY IN MIND

Whenever you're funneling data between multiple systems, **security** is a top concern. The last thing you want is to unintentionally expose user info or allow requests that your Bubble app can't handle safely. Besides hiding your API credentials, consider these points:

- **HTTPS Only:** Make sure any external API call is done via an encrypted SSL/TLS connection (https://). This helps prevent data interception.
- **Privacy Roles on Data:** If you're saving external API responses to your database, confirm that only the correct user roles can see or modify them.
- **Validate Responses:** Check for unexpected data before displaying it. Some APIs may return an error or partial data, so adding conditional checks in your workflows can prevent displaying broken content.

LOOKING AHEAD

Building robust API connections is like unlocking a universal translator for your app, letting you tap into countless services, data sources, and functionalities. Once you get comfortable with the concept of API calls, you may find yourself streamlining processes in ways you never thought possible, from automating routine tasks to creating interactive dashboards that reflect up-to-the-minute information.

If there's one concept I hope you take away from this chapter, it's that integrating external APIs can be both straightforward and powerful. Bubble's visual interface conceals the complexities of network requests, JSON parsing, and token management, leaving you free to focus on what matters most: your users and the value your app provides. And once your app becomes an orchestration of multiple services, you'll see just how limitless the no-code approach can be.

Chapter 9: Managing Plugins and Integrations

I still remember how thrilling it felt the first time I discovered that Bubble's ecosystem offer plugins for practically every challenge I faced. From in-depth payment handling to adding robust chart libraries, plugins opened a new world of possibilities and saved me from reinventing the wheel. In this chapter, I'll share my experience navigating the plugin landscape, highlight key steps for installation, and offer practical pointers on maintaining a smooth, hassle-free relationship with each integration you include in your app.

UNDERSTANDING THE PLUGIN ECOSYSTEM

Bubble's plugin marketplace is both vast and ever-evolving. New solutions for analytics, email marketing, design elements, and dozens more appear frequently. You can explore this plugin ecosystem by heading to the "Plugins" section in your Bubble Editor. Once there, you'll see a search bar, a list of recommended extensions, and various categories to help locate what you need. It can feel overwhelming at first, but that volume of choice is also where the true power lies—you'll often find a ready-made solution for the exact feature you've envisioned.

CHOOSING THE RIGHT PLUGIN

While browsing through all those options, you might notice certain plugins do similar tasks. To settle on the best fit, I generally follow these considerations:

- **User Ratings and Reviews:** Comments from other Bubblers can give honest insights into a plugin's performance and any quirks. I often check the date of recent reviews, as up-to-date feedback suggests the plugin is actively maintained.
- **Plugin Author and Support:** Sometimes an official company publishes a plugin; other times it's built by an independent developer. I pay attention to support channels—like documentation, email addresses, or a forum thread—so I know where to turn if something goes wrong.
- **Features vs. Complexity:** A plugin offering more advanced capabilities might also introduce heavier configuration steps. If my needs are basic, I might opt for a lightweight alternative that's easier to maintain.
- **Compatibility and Version Updates:** Some plugins explicitly state Bubble version requirements or mention known conflicts with other plugins. Checking these details ahead of time saves headaches later.

INSTALLING AND CONFIGURING PLUGINS

Installing a plugin in Bubble is delightfully straightforward. In the "Plugins" tab, clicking the "Add plugins" button reveals the marketplace. Once I spot a plugin that meets my needs, I select "Install"—and just like that, it appears in my app's plugin list. If the plugin needs extra setup, Bubble will present a configuration page asking for API keys or account IDs. Here's an example of what you might do after installation:

1. **Enter Credentials:** If you're connecting a payment provider, paste your published key and secret key in the designated fields.
2. **Set Default Options:** Some plugins let you define default behaviors—like currency formats or default chart layouts—so the plugin integrates smoothly into your design.
3. **Check Documentation:** Many plugin authors include a guide or documentation link, which is essential for advanced configurations or troubleshooting.

Once configured, new elements or workflow actions associated with the plugin will appear in your app's editor. For instance, if it's an analytics plugin, you could see new workflow actions such as "Track Event" or options to embed reporting dashboards directly on a page.

ALIGNING PLUGINS WITH YOUR WORKFLOWS

After installation, the real fun begins when you incorporate these tools into your workflows. Let's say you installed a plugin to send instant push notifications. You could create a workflow step that triggers a push message when a new piece of content is posted, or when a user completes a certain action in your app. In my projects, this synergy between plugin capabilities and Bubble's no-code logic felt almost limitless.

One tip is to treat a plugin's feature set like any other part of your editor. In "Workflow" view, you'll notice relevant plugin actions listed under categories or by searching for keywords. You can chain multiple plugin actions, like calculating analytics metrics, then updating your database, and finally displaying a summary on the screen. Each new integration you install broadens the scope of what you can achieve visually and logically—without writing scripts yourself.

SECURITY AND PLUGIN PERMISSIONS

Amid the ease of installing external tools, I always keep a watchful eye on security and data access. Some plugins require deeper access to user information, so it's wise to confirm you're comfortable sharing that data. For instance, if you connect to a plugin that manages mailing lists, you'll be exposing user email addresses to a third-party service.

To handle this safely, I prefer to:

- **Read the Plugin's Privacy Policy:** Make sure it aligns with your own compliance requirements if you're dealing with sensitive data.
- **Scope Down Your Data Usage:** Only feed the plugin the minimum level of information required for it to function. Instead of sending the entire user record, pass just their email address or name.

- **Review Bubble Privacy Rules:** Check your Data Privacy settings to see if the plugin could inadvertently expose data to unauthorized users.

By controlling how data moves between Bubble and any plugin, you'll maintain tighter control over your user's trust and adherence to relevant regulations.

KEEPING PLUGINS UP-TO-DATE

Plugin creators release updates for bug fixes or new features, which Bubble flags with an "Update available" label in your app's plugin list. Clicking "Update" brings in the latest code. Though it's quick to do, I often test these updates on a non-production version first. Occasionally, plugin changes can break existing setups or introduce new fields that require additional configuration.

Here's my mini-process before I hit "Update":

1. **Create a Test Version:** Duplicate or branch your app to a staging area where you can safely update the plugin without risking your live environment.
2. **Validate Critical Workflows:** Run through essential user paths—sign-ups, purchases, or any flows relying on the plugin's functionality.
3. **Check for Deprecations:** Skim the plugin's release notes to see if they ended support for certain methods or changed naming conventions.
4. **Deploy to Live:** Once everything passes testing, merge your changes and update the plugin in production.

This methodical approach has saved me from the occasional headache of discovering mid-launch that a plugin's new version doesn't behave exactly as before.

MANAGING MULTIPLE INTEGRATIONS

For larger Bubble projects, you might juggle many plugins, and that can lead to clutter or confusion if not managed correctly. My approach to staying organized includes:

- **Naming Conventions:** If the plugin adds new custom states or elements, I'll prefix them with the plugin name—like "Zapier-Trigger" or "Stripe-Payment." This helps distinguish them from native Bubble elements.
- **Periodic Cleanups:** Sometimes I install a plugin just to test a concept. If it doesn't fit my needs, I remove it to minimize the risk of future conflicts or overhead.
- **Cross-Plugin Conflicts:** When two plugins govern similar features—like multiple date picker plugins—I disable or uninstall the one I'm not actively using, to avoid messing up user experience.

By adopting a consistent naming strategy and revisiting plugin usage occasionally, the entire architecture of your app remains more transparent and easier to troubleshoot.

EXPLORING THIRD-PARTY AUTOMATION PLATFORMS

Beyond Bubble's native marketplace, you may also hear about automation tools like Zapier, Make, or Tray.io that coordinate data flow between many different web apps. In some cases, these platforms can serve as a go-between for Bubble and other services that don't yet have a dedicated Bubble plugin. For instance, you can trigger a "Zap" every time a user submits a form in Bubble. That Zap could then pass the data to a customer relationship management tool. Or the other way around—if a new lead appears in your CRM, you initiate a workflow in Bubble to create a matching user record. While these setups do require some additional steps, they help fill in gaps where a direct plugin might not exist.

WHEN TO CONSIDER BUILDING A CUSTOM PLUGIN

Sometimes, you won't find a pre-built solution that matches your vision perfectly, or the existing plugin might feel cumbersome for your specific scenario. In such cases, Bubble allows you to create **custom plugins**. While this does require some coding knowledge—particularly JavaScript—Bubble's plugin editor offers a structured way to define new elements, actions, or data connections. If you or someone on your team is comfortable handling scripts, building a custom integration can be well worth the effort, especially if:

- You need a proprietary service integrated securely.
- You want absolute control over how an integration handles data and error states.
- You'd like to share or even monetize your work by publishing the plugin to Bubble's marketplace.

ENSURING LONG-TERM STABILITY

Integrations can make or break an app's reliability. When an external service hiccups, your users might see broken features or error messages. While you can't always control external dependencies, you *can* brace for potential disruptions by:

1. **Displaying Graceful Fallbacks:** If a plugin fails to load data, present a friendly message or partial results instead of a hard error.
2. **Watching Service Status:** For critical plugins, periodically check the provider's status page or subscribe to update notifications.
3. **Testing Recovery:** Simulate outages. Uninstall or disable the plugin in a staging environment to see how your app behaves. This helps you quickly fix issues when a real outage occurs.

A thoughtful approach to potential downtime helps maintain trust with your user base, proving you're prepared across all fronts.

CELEBRATING THE POWER OF COLLABORATION

One of the things I most appreciate about working with plugins is the sense of community that grows around shared challenges. If you ever feel stuck—maybe the official documentation only covers the basics—chances are you'll find other Bubble builders who've tackled the same obstacle. Forums, user groups, or direct contact with the developer can open doors to new techniques, custom code snippets, or creative ways to extend an existing plugin's capabilities.

FINAL THOUGHTS ON PLUGINS AND INTEGRATIONS

Embedding the right tools into a Bubble application can dramatically amplify your app's impact. Rather than coding entire payment portals or advanced charting libraries from scratch, you can simply install a plugin, fine-tune the settings, and harness that functionality in moments. Each new integration you master not only optimizes your build time but also broadens the horizons of what your no-code creations can accomplish.

That said, thoughtful management is key—knowing why you add each plugin, keeping your list tidy, and verifying security measures. This deliberate approach lets you strike the perfect balance between convenience and control. As your comfort with Bubble deepens, you may find yourself even creating custom plugins to address gaps you encounter, turning your expertise into solutions the entire community can benefit from.

With an organized mindset and a bit of curiosity, managing plugins and integrations becomes second nature. Take the time to explore this vibrant aspect of Bubble's ecosystem, and you'll soon see how it accelerates your path from idea to execution—no coding required.

Chapter 10: Working with Reusable Elements

WHY REUSABLE ELEMENTS MATTER

Early in my Bubble journey, I was excited when I realized I could streamline my app design with reusable elements. Instead of manually copying and pasting the same header, footer, or form across multiple pages, I discovered that I could create a master element once and then reuse it wherever needed. In my experience, this approach saves enormous time, ensures consistency, and makes updating global pieces of the interface far simpler. For anyone aiming to maintain a professional look without duplicating effort, reusable elements quickly become a must-have skill in the Bubble toolbox.

CREATING YOUR FIRST REUSABLE ELEMENT

To create a reusable element, I navigate to the top menu in the Bubble Editor, where there's an option labeled "Add a new reusable element." Once selected, Bubble prompts me to name it—something like "Main Header" or "Login Form." I like to keep these names straightforward, so I know at a glance what the element contains. As soon as I confirm, Bubble takes me into a dedicated editing environment that feels nearly identical to designing a regular page, except this workspace is solely focused on the element itself. This separation makes it easier for me to manage the appearance and functionality without accidentally changing page-level designs.

STRUCTURING LAYOUT AND STYLE

From a design perspective, I treat my reusable just like any other page section. I can add text, buttons, icons, images, or input fields—whatever is essential to fulfill its purpose. For instance, if I'm building a navigation bar, I might include a logo image on the left, a series of text links or icons in the center, and a profile menu on the right. Once arranged, I can apply consistent fonts, colors, and sizes, so that every instance of the header retains the same branding.

One tip I've picked up is to place container elements (like groups) within the reusable to keep related items together. This structure not only helps keep the editor tidy but also allows me to adjust entire sections of the reusable without individually dragging each element around later.

INCORPORATING WORKFLOWS INTO REUSABLES

Reusable elements aren't just about attractive interfaces—I've found they're also a powerful way to embed logic. Let's say I have a reusable login form. I can build all the necessary workflows (such as verifying credentials or redirecting users once they log in) inside the reusable itself. This way, whenever I drop that login form on a page, the underlying actions come with it. That consistency is huge. If I want to update the flow—maybe add a new security check—I only need to make the change once inside the reusable element. The modifications ripple across every page where it's used.

At times, I've needed to pass specific data back and forth between a reusable and the parent page. In those situations, I rely on "Custom states" or "Inputs" on the reusable side, which act like placeholders for any data I want the parent page workflows to work with. This design pattern keeps everything neatly modular: the reusable focuses on what it does best, while the parent page retains broader control of the entire app context.

PLACING REUSABLE ELEMENTS IN YOUR APP

Once I've crafted the perfect reusable element, adding it to a page is straightforward. In the editor's "Design" tab, I spot the reusable element in the list of available page components. From there, it's a simple drag-and-drop motion to place it where I want. I can resize it as needed, though I typically match it to the space I originally envisioned—like a site-wide header spanning the full width for a desktop interface.

Sometimes, I embed multiple instances of the same reusable on a single page, each in different sections or with slightly different data flows. As an example, if I use a card-style reusable element to display user stats, I could place it in both a sidebar and a main content area, adjusting each instance's custom state or data source to highlight different metrics. Seeing how it all comes together on one page gives me a real sense of the reusable's flexibility.

EDITING AND UPDATING REUSABLES

I love how Bubble centralizes changes to a reusable element. If I decide to tweak a color, rearrange buttons, or refine a workflow, I open the reusable itself, make the edits, and Bubble applies those changes automatically wherever I've placed it. This approach saves me the headache of updating each individual page for something as small as a font style adjustment. It's also a major confidence booster—I know that users get the latest version of the interface no matter where they navigate in my app.

Of course, there are times when I want a page-specific variation. Maybe the form fields or button labels differ slightly on one page. In that case, I'll create a separate reusable that's almost identical to the original, and label it distinctly. That way, I keep my customization in check without cluttering the main reusable's design.

ADVANCED TECHNIQUES: NESTING AND CONTEXTUAL DATA

If you've ever tried to build something like a multi-layered menu, you may find yourself wanting to place a reusable inside another reusable. This can happen if you have a universal header that also needs a specialized sub-menu in different app sections. I recall being cautious the first time I nested a reusable, but I quickly realized Bubble handles the hierarchy well. It's crucial, however, to be thoughtful with naming and data passing—an element nested too deeply can cause confusion if you're not consistent in how you label states or reference them in workflows.

Another scenario that pops up for me is using conditional logic based on contextual data. For example, a sidebar reusable might display slightly different navigation options if the viewer is an admin. By leveraging conditional statements and referencing "Current user's role" at the reusable level, I can tailor what users see without rewriting my entire menu. It's a small detail that helps keep the interface clean and relevant to the user's permissions.

VERSION CONTROL AND TESTING

Any time I experiment with a major redesign—say, introducing a brand-new look to a universal header—I prefer to test it on a staging version of my app. This way, if the changes don't sit well with user feedback or break something unexpectedly, I can revert to the previous iteration without impacting the live version. Once I'm satisfied everything works, I merge those changes into production.

For thorough testing, I like to preview multiple pages that use the reusable. It's easy to overlook subtle interaction points in a single test. By stepping through various pages and scenarios, I catch small quirks—like misaligned items or workflows that fail under certain conditions—before pushing it all live.

PRACTICAL EXAMPLES OF REUSABLES

Site Header & **Footer:** Arguably the most common use case, ensuring every page keeps consistent branding.

Forms & Pop-ups: Perfect for reusable login forms, sign-up prompts, or feedback modals. **User Profile Card:** Display key user details anywhere in the app—just set the data source to the relevant user record. **Dashboard Widgets:** Show charts, stats, or tables that tap into your data. This works nicely for big apps with multiple analytics pages.

MAINTAINING CONSISTENCY

Before I started using reusable elements, my app designs sometimes suffered from tiny inconsistencies—margins off by a few pixels, slightly different colors, or mismatched fonts. It was easy to overlook these details when copying elements across pages manually. Reusables helped me lock down a standard format that persists everywhere it appears. If I need to adjust something, I make a single change, and suddenly my whole app aligns to that new standard. This consistency not only looks more professional but also makes user navigation more intuitive.

COMMON MISTAKES TO AVOID

Overcomplicating a Single Reusable: I've been tempted to stuff every feature into a huge header or multi-purpose form, which can make it unwieldy. Splitting large elements into more targeted pieces often streamlines the workflow. **Forgetting Dynamic Data Fields:** If your reusable references data that doesn't exist on certain pages, it can throw errors or appear blank. Ensuring each parent page feeds proper data prevents awkward gaps. **Ignoring Mobile Responsiveness:** Reusables can be just as responsive as any other Bubble page, but it's easy to forget to test smaller screen sizes. A well-crafted responsive design keeps your element flexible across all devices.

EMBRACING THE REUSABLE MINDSET

As I became more comfortable working with reusables, I started thinking of my app in modular chunks. Each chunk, or reusable, has a clear purpose—like navigation, user forms, or specialized displays. This perspective encourages me to keep my designs organized, my workflows focused, and my layouts uncluttered. If you approach your project by identifying repeat patterns early on, you'll discover that the entire build process becomes more strategic and efficient.

From experience, I've seen how reusables reduce not just development time but also ongoing maintenance costs. They're among the unsung heroes of Bubble development—flipping the script from manual repetition to systemized consistency. If you're striving to create a polished, maintainable app, it's well worth your time to build a library of well-crafted reusable elements that can evolve along with your ideas.

Chapter 11:
Responsiveness and
Mobile-Friendly Design

When I started building my very first Bubble application, I was surprised by how quickly I could get a desktop layout up and running. Yet the moment I tested that same layout on my phone, things looked cramped and elements didn't stack well. That's when I realized that having a great mobile-friendly interface is just as crucial as looking good on a large screen. In this chapter, I'll walk through the essentials of Bubble's responsiveness tools, as well as show you how to ensure every page in your app scales gracefully across the countless devices and screen sizes your users will be using.

UNDERSTANDING THE IMPORTANCE OF RESPONSIVE DESIGN

In my experience, responsive design isn't just about rearranging elements to fit a small screen—it's about offering a seamless user journey whether someone is accessing your site from a phone, tablet, or desktop. I've seen well-crafted responsive apps instill a sense of trust and professionalism, while disorganized mobile layouts can quickly drive users away. With Bubble's responsive engine, it's entirely possible to create fluid layouts that adapt automatically to any viewport.

THE RESPONSIVE EDITOR: A QUICK TOUR

Whenever I need to fine-tune how a page displays at various sizes, I switch over to Bubble's responsive editor. At first glance, the interface can be a bit overwhelming, but it's neatly organized with control panels for setting minimum or maximum widths, margins, and alignment rules. On the main screen, there's a slider or breakpoints that let me simulate how my app appears when smaller or wider.

I usually start by dragging this slider to see how my design shifts. If elements overlap or get cut off at a certain width, it's an obvious sign I need to adjust some settings. The visual feedback is immediate, helping me catch issues fast and assemble a layout that can scale without frustration.

KEY RESPONSIVE SETTINGS

In my own implementations, a few settings in Bubble have been game-changers for getting layouts right. Here's what I rely on most often:

- **Container Layout:** Choices like "Fixed," "Align to parent," or "Row" and "Column" configurations define how elements position themselves within their container. I pay special attention to row and column arrangements because they help content adjust fluidly when screens shrink.
- **Min/Max Width:** For each group or element, I can set a minimum or maximum width. A typical

approach I use is to give buttons a min width (so they never collapse into unreadable shapes) and let text stretches fill the extra space up to a certain point, so lines don't become excessively long.

- **Margin and Padding:** Managing spacing around elements ensures content doesn't become cramped or too spread out at different breakpoints. I find consistent margins give pages a more unified feel.
- **Collapse When Hidden:** This nifty feature is perfect for optional sidebars or things like advanced filtering panels that you want to disappear entirely on mobile. If an element is set to collapse, it won't leave awkward white space behind when toggled off.

USING ROWS AND COLUMNS EFFECTIVELY

One shift in my mindset with Bubble's new responsive engine was thinking more in terms of rows and columns rather than individual fixed positions. When I place elements within a column container, for example, I know they'll automatically stack vertically on narrower screens. Likewise, row containers help align items side by side, and they wrap nicely if spacing gets tight. This methodology, sometimes referred to as "flexbox" in traditional web design, ensures I'm building layouts that can elegantly rearrange themselves without tedious micromanagement.

For example, take a product listing card on a marketplace app: the image can appear on the left with details on the right while on desktop, but on portrait phones, everything can stack neatly in a column. By leveraging columns, I let

Bubble handle that transition for me, so I don't have to create separate elements for each device type.

MANAGING COMPLEX LAYOUTS WITH GROUPS

When first working on a new screen, I group elements that belong together—like a user avatar, name, and role—so I can treat them as a single unit when adjusting responsive rules. For instance, if I want a profile block to shrink proportionally, I enable responsive settings on its parent group. Having a clear hierarchy of groups keeps me from messing with each small element individually later on.

It also helps to toggle "Make this element fixed-width" on or off at the group level, depending on how flexible I need that segment to be. If I'm aiming for a full-width hero banner, I might set the group to stretch across the page at all times, whereas a button or logo might remain fixed in size for branding consistency.

DEALING WITH IMAGES AND VIDEO

Images or embedded media can be tricky in responsive design. If I don't set them up properly, they can overflow their container or shrink awkwardly. In Bubble, I typically set images to "keep aspect ratio" so they scale proportionally and maintain clarity. That way, whether someone checks my app on a watch-like screen or a cinematic ultra-wide monitor, the images look properly sized without distortion.

For background images, I pay special attention to the "image position" or "background style" settings. Depending on the page design, sometimes I need the image to center, or I might want it to scale so the focal point remains visible at different breakpoints. Fine-tuning these minor details can vastly improve an app's visual polish.

BREAKPOINTS AND CONDITIONAL FORMATTING

While Bubble's layout engine handles most scenarios with ease, there are moments when I want more precise control. Maybe I want a certain sidebar to vanish entirely when the viewport is narrower than 600 pixels. For these cases, I use conditional statements—like "When current page width < 600, this element is not visible." I'll also switch text sizes to something bigger on extremely small screens or let a hero banner's font shrink to avoid horizontal scrolling.

Thinking about each chunk of my layout as "Does it need special rules below a certain breakpoint?" helps me be proactive. By systematically adding conditions for my main breakpoints (mobile, tablet, desktop), I rarely run into scenarios where the design falls apart for certain users.

TESTING ACROSS DEVICES

No matter how good the preview in Bubble's editor might look, I've learned first-hand the importance of real-device testing. I typically check my project on at least one smartphone, one tablet-sized device or simulator, and one desktop browser. In particular, I watch for:

- **Touch targets:** Buttons and input fields should be large enough to tap without zooming in.
- **Readability:** Text that grows or shrinks proportionately for consistent line spacing on mobile, especially for multi-line descriptions.
- **Scrolling impact:** Certain elements might inadvertently create side scrolling on small screens if I forgot to set a group to collapse or adjust its max width.

If something seems "off," I return to the responsive editor or add a new condition. This cycle of previewing, testing, and tweaking might feel slow at first, but it's usually the fastest route to a polished final product.

COMMON PITFALLS AND HOW TO AVOID THEM

Pitfall	Solution

101

Overlapping Elements	Use row and column containers wherever possible and allow automatic wrapping. Manually layering items often leads to collisions on smaller screens.
Fixed Width Overuse	If every element is stuck at a fixed size, your layout won't adapt. Reserve fixed widths for logos or minimal icons; let the rest expand or shrink to fit.
Ignoring Padding	Forget to space out elements, and they'll clash visually. Always set comfortable margins or padding so content stays readable on smaller displays.
Forgetting Orientation	Many users browse in landscape mode. Check both orientations to confirm your design remains stable and legible.

FOCUSING ON PERFORMANCE

Another aspect of mobile-friendly design is performance. If a page takes forever to load on a phone, no amount of beautiful responsive layout can salvage the user's experience. While Bubble's hosting is generally efficient, I keep an eye on large images or background videos that can strain bandwidth on mobile connections. Optimizing image sizes or using compressed media can go a long way in speeding up page load times. Additionally, I aim to simplify data retrieval so that each screen only fetches what's absolutely needed, preventing the app from becoming sluggish on weaker devices.

ITERATIVE REFINEMENT

Once my pages look decent on all test devices, I don't consider the process finished. I usually gather feedback from a few users, especially if I'm deploying an app with a broader audience. They might point out that certain text is still too small or a button is too close to the screen edge for comfortable tapping. Each iteration helps me fine-tune that user experience until the layout feels natural, no matter the device size or orientation.

FINAL THOUGHTS

Designing for responsiveness in Bubble is an ongoing process of balancing structure, flexibility, and user expectations. When I embrace the tools Bubble provides—like rows, columns, conditional breakpoints, and layered groups—it feels empowering to see my app adapt on screens both large and small. And while it may be tempting to overlook smaller devices at first, I've learned that catering to mobile usage can significantly widen my audience and strengthen user satisfaction overall.

With a careful approach and a commitment to testing, any Bubble creator can deliver a polished, mobile-friendly app that retains its core style and functionality across the full spectrum of devices. After all, users will notice the difference when your app "just works" on any screen, and so will you when feedback and engagement soar as a direct result.

Chapter 12: Visual Design and Styling Best Practices

The first time I attempted to create a more refined, professional look for my Bubble app, I realized good design isn't just about adding pretty colors or fancy fonts. It's about crafting an experience that looks cohesive, communicates my brand identity, and guides users intuitively through each page. Over time, I've discovered a set of best practices that greatly simplify the visual design process—while ensuring my app stands out in a polished, consistent way.

DEFINING A CLEAR DESIGN LANGUAGE

An important lesson I learned was to define a basic design language before worrying about the intricate details. Think of this as the "DNA" of your application's look and feel. It includes:

- **Color Palette:** Choose a set of compatible colors—primary, secondary, accent, and neutral shades. Selecting four or five colors ensures you have enough variety without overwhelming the interface.
- **Typography:** Decide on no more than two or three fonts. Usually, one for headers or titles, and another for body text. Matching weights and sizes consistently across pages reduces the impression of clutter.
- **Visual Elements:** Icons, shapes, or illustration styles can reinforce a cohesive theme. Pick a style—flat icons, doodle-style sketches, or sleek silhouettes—and use it consistently.

Once you define these core elements, you have a guiding compass for all your design choices. I've found that sticking to the original plan helps avoid second-guessing every color or shape down the line, freeing me up to concentrate on the app's functionality.

WORKING WITH THE STYLE TAB

Bubble's **Style** tab is one of my favorite tools for ensuring consistency. Instead of modifying each element's properties individually, I create and edit universal styles—like a "Button Primary" style or a "Body Text" style. This approach centralizes design updates. If I later decide to switch my primary color from royal blue to teal, I can change it in one place, and every button style in my app automatically updates.

When I name these styles, I try to be explicit. For instance, "Header H1 – Blue" or "Button – Danger/Red Background." Clear naming helps me identify what each style is meant for. Moreover, if I'm working with a partner or a design-savvy teammate, descriptive labels make it much easier for others to jump in and keep design usage consistent.

LEVERAGING VISUAL HIERARCHY

Understanding and applying **visual hierarchy** can dramatically improve how users digest information on each page. Elements at the top of this hierarchy—like headlines or important calls-to-action—should be more prominent, often through size, color contrast, or positioning. Supporting details can be smaller or use less distinct colors, ensuring they don't distract from the primary message.

Here's a quick example I rely on often: a sign-up screen. I place the headline or key marketing line at the top in bold text, maybe even a brighter color. Underneath, subtle text can describe the benefits of signing up, and the main button stands out again with a strong accent color. By contrasting the main components, I guide the user's eye exactly where I want them to look first—improving clarity and efficiency.

BALANCING WHITE SPACE

One of the easiest ways to give your app a more polished feel is through the proper use of white space (or negative space). Early on, I tended to cram too many elements together, anxious about leaving "unused" screen real estate. Over time, I realized white space actually boosts readability and adds a sense of sophistication.

To incorporate white space effectively, I define consistent margins and paddings around text blocks, buttons, images, or input fields. This spacing acts as a natural buffer between elements, so the interface never feels claustrophobic. It might take a bit of testing in Bubble's editor, but the result is a clean, modern layout where each piece of content has the room it needs to shine.

COLOR CONTRAST AND ACCESSIBILITY

As I became more mindful of user experiences, I also started thinking about accessibility. Ensuring sufficient color contrast between text and backgrounds is crucial. For instance, if your background is a light gray, you might opt for a deep charcoal text color instead of medium gray. This difference helps visually impaired or colorblind users, and it also improves general clarity for everyone.

Auto-checking contrast ratios is one of my best practices. Several free contrast checker tools online can tell you if your chosen text and background colors are accessible or not. It might feel like an extra step, but it pays off in an inclusive design that doesn't inadvertently exclude any segment of users.

USING IMAGES AND ICONS WISELY

Visuals can enrich your design in many ways. I try to select images or icons that complement the topic of each page. Generic stock photos can dilute your brand identity if they appear random or out of context. Instead, picking curated, cohesive visuals that align with your brand colors and style can reinforce the app's theme.

I also like to keep icon styles consistent. Mixing flat icons, skeuomorphic icons, and line-art icons together can become distracting. Whether you choose a minimalist outline or filled shape approach, stay consistent so the interface appears polished and thought-out. Bubble lets you easily upload custom icons—just remember to keep them aligned to your overall design language.

TAILORING FONTS FOR READABILITY

Picking high-quality typography is more than a style choice: it directly affects legibility and the user's overall impression. In Bubble, it's easy to import custom fonts or select from the built-in Google Fonts library. While unconventional typefaces might look trendy, it's vital to consider whether they'll hinder readability over multiple paragraphs. If you're using a decorative font for headings, pair it with a clean, sans-serif font for longer content.

Additionally, I pay attention to line spacing and font sizes. Too little spacing in large text blocks can strain the reader's eyes, while too much spacing can make the interface look sparse. Testing these variations on different screen sizes—desktop, tablet, mobile—helps me confirm that my font choices remain legible everywhere.

CONSISTENCY ACROSS PAGES

In the early days, I tended to treat each new page as a blank canvas, experimenting wildly with design ideas. The outcome was often a series of disconnected pages that felt more like patchwork than a cohesive app. Users would see shifting button shapes or mismatched form styling from page to page, which undermined the sense of professionalism.

Now, I plan out repeating components—like headings, buttons, and form inputs—using Bubble's styles to keep every page aligned. Headers, footers, and navigation bars remain consistent, so no matter where a user goes in my app, they have visual markers that feel familiar. After all, design consistency is not only about aesthetics but also about orienting users so they don't have to relearn navigation cues on each new screen.

PRACTICING RESPONSIVE-FRIENDLY STYLING

Part of good styling means anticipating how elements reshape themselves on smaller screens or unusual aspect ratios. Before finalizing my design, I usually take a quick look at how headings, images, and buttons appear in mobile layout previews. If text gets cut off or backgrounds lose alignment, I adjust margins or switch the sizing rules. That way, my styling remains unified whether viewed on a desktop or a phone.

Bubble's conditional formatting also helps me adapt certain design features for mobile. For instance, if a large hero header is overwhelming on a phone, I might set a condition that reduces font size or hides non-essential flourishes below a specific screen width. It's an elegant way to maintain brand consistency while respecting the constraints of smaller displays.

ITERATION AND FEEDBACK

One invaluable piece of advice I've stuck with is to seek feedback on design throughout the build, not just at the end. Sometimes, details that seem logical to me—like a vibrant accent color—might come across as too harsh for others. A quick user test or a peer review can reveal whether certain styling choices distract or confuse end-users.

When I gather feedback, I aim for specifics: "Is the new color scheme comfortable to look at, or does it strain your eyes?" or "Do you find the button text easy to read against the background?" The more direct the question, the more actionable the feedback becomes. Then, with each iteration, my overall styling gets sharper and more user-centered.

MAINTAINING A STYLE GUIDE

Finally, I recommend documenting your styling rules in a basic **Style Guide**. Even if it's just a brief page listing your brand palette hex codes, preferred font sizes, and standard button styles, having a reference helps you or your collaborators stay on track. Over time, if new features demand fresh color variations or additional text styling, you can update this guide so the rest of the app continues to feel cohesive. It's much easier than trying to remember every detail from memory, especially as an app grows in complexity.

BRINGING IT ALL TOGETHER

Visual design in Bubble combines both creativity and structure. By establishing a clear design language, leveraging the Style tab, and paying attention to details like hierarchy, color contrasts, and typography, you can elevate your app from functional to truly engaging. The best part is that with Bubble's configuration options, changes can propagate effortlessly across your entire app—so your energy can stay focused on user experience rather than repetitive styling tasks.

With a little strategic thought and a focus on consistent execution, you'll discover that visual design isn't an afterthought or a chore—it's a powerful way to reinforce your brand, guide users through your app, and earn their confidence. The more you refine these best practices, the easier it becomes to craft an interface that feels just as intuitive as it looks.

Chapter 13: Custom States and Dynamic Behavior

UNDERSTANDING THE POWER OF CUSTOM STATES

When I first started building apps in Bubble, I was intrigued by how easily I could connect visual elements to data entries in the database. But once I discovered **custom states**, it felt like I'd unlocked an entirely new dimension of interactivity. Custom states let you store values directly on an element (or the page itself) without constantly writing data to the database. As a result, I could create highly responsive features—like showing and hiding pop-ups, toggling between different views, or holding temporary input selections—that didn't require hitting the server or cluttering my database tables. Think of custom states as small memory slots or variables that your app can update and reference instantly.

What's truly remarkable is how intuitive the process can be. You pick the element that will hold the state, name the state, choose its data type (text, number, yes/no, list, etc.), and that's it. From then on, you can set and retrieve that state's value anywhere in your workflows or conditional formatting. It might sound simple, but these small building blocks can create dynamic, real-time experiences without writing a single line of code.

WHY CUSTOM STATES ARE SO USEFUL

One question that often pops up is: "Why not just put everything in the database?" While storing persistent data in the database is essential for user-generated content or records, it also introduces overhead. Pulling from or writing to the database usually triggers page refreshes, increases load times, and can muddy your data with temporary pieces of information that aren't truly needed long-term.

To me, custom states represent a lighter, more flexible approach. If you need to briefly save a user's preference (like filter options for a search) or hold a small piece of text to display in a tooltip, there's no reason to create a brand-new field in your database just for that. A custom state is stored locally in the user's browser session, which means it's fast and ephemeral. When the user navigates away from the page, the custom state disappears, making sense for anything that doesn't warrant permanent storage.

CREATING AND ASSIGNING A STATE

To give you a feel for how it works, here's my usual workflow for setting up a state:

1. **Select an Element:** I often choose the page itself if multiple components need easy access to the same state. Alternatively, I might pick a specific group or reusable element if the state only matters there.
2. **Add a New Custom State:** In the element's Properties panel (or by right-clicking the element in the Elements Tree), I click "Add a custom state."
3. **Name the State and Set a Type:** For instance, I might name it "showDetails" and select "yes/no" as the type if the goal is to toggle a detailed info panel on or off.
4. **Initialize the State (Optional):** You can set a default value, such as "no" for a toggle or an empty list for multi-value states. This step isn't always required, but it's handy if you have a known starting point.

Once defined, the state is ready to be manipulated anywhere on that page. Whenever I want to change that value—for example, flipping "showDetails" from "no" to "yes"—I create a workflow action: "Element > Set State." I choose the element that holds the state, pick the specific state, and define the new value. In just a single workflow step, I can alter the app's behavior without touching the database.

USING CUSTOM STATES IN WORKFLOWS

After you've created a custom state, the fun begins when you incorporate it into your workflows. Let's say I've got a button labeled "Toggle Info." When the user clicks it, I might have a workflow that sets "showDetails" to "yes" if it's currently "no" (or vice versa). Then, in the conditionals for a group containing extra details, I can say, "When showDetails is yes, this group is visible." Just like that, I've built a collapsible information panel without storing anything in the database.

Beyond basic toggles, I frequently use states to store intermediate values in multi-step workflows. For example, if I'm building a form wizard with multiple sections, I'll keep track of the current section number or label in a custom state. Each time the user clicks "Next," the custom state increments by 1, and the design reacts by revealing the appropriate section. This flexibility ensures the transitions happen quickly and smoothly, giving the appearance of a single, dynamic screen rather than multiple pages.

COMBINING STATES WITH CONDITIONAL FORMATTING

One of my favorite aspects of Bubble is how easy it is to connect conditions to just about anything—visibility, color, text, or even animation. Whenever I store a value in a custom state, it becomes an option in the conditional editor for any element. This might look like:

"When [Element's Custom State] is [some value], change background color to highlight."

Because conditions update in real time, it creates the impression that the app is responding instantly to user actions. A practical example is a tabbed interface: I set a custom state called "currentTab" and then define conditions on each tab's content group to only display when "currentTab = X." Instead of jumping around pages, the user sees instant changes smoothly within one interface.

WORKING WITH LISTS IN CUSTOM STATES

While single-value states are common for toggling or storing small bits of info, **list states** open a world of possibilities. Suppose I have a repeating group of products, and I want to let users select multiple items before performing an action (such as adding them to a cart or marking them as favorites). I can create a custom state that stores a list of "Product" data type.

Any time a user checks a box next to a product, a workflow updates the custom state, adding or removing that product from the list. At the end, I can reference that entire list in a "Bulk Action" workflow, saving the items to the database, emailing them, or anything else the app demands. Because the list exists purely in memory, I avoid writing partial changes to the database until the user is truly finished, leading to a cleaner record of final selections.

PRACTICAL EXAMPLES OF CUSTOM STATE USAGE

Toggle UI Elements: My most frequent use is toggling pop-ups, sidebars, or hidden sections. A yes/no state makes it effortless to show or hide these components based on clicks.

Filters and Sorting: When building dynamic searches or advanced filters, I store the selected filter options in states. My repeating group references these states to conditionally display   updated   results.

Multi-Step Forms: I track the user's position in the form using a numeric or text-based state, switching forms on the fly.

Storing Temporary Counts or Totals: If I need to show a running total of items in a session cart before saving them, I keep these smaller calculations in a number state for immediate updates.

PUSHING BOUNDARIES WITH STATES AND WORKFLOWS

Custom states don't just limit themselves to simple toggles or storing text. You can integrate them with analytics, animations, or even conditional transitions. If you're aiming for a polished, application-like feel, you can store page navigation states (like "Home," "Profile," "Messages") and swap content areas on the exact same page, giving the illusion of a single-page app.

I've also experimented with combining states and the "Schedule a custom event" feature for advanced interactions. For instance, I might set a state to track how many seconds have passed since a user completed a certain action, then show a custom alert if they remain inactive. This type of ephemeral data is perfect for states because it resets cleanly once they leave the page or refresh the browser.

BEST PRACTICES AND COMMON PITFALLS

- **Name States Clearly:** If you have multiple states scattered across elements, it's easy to lose track. I keep a clear naming convention, like "cartItemsList" or "dashboardToggle," to quickly recognize their roles.
- **Don't Overuse Short-Lived States:** While states are really flexible, too many overlapping states can make debugging a headache. If you're saving data that needs to persist beyond a single session, or across multiple pages, a database record is still the safer approach.
- **Verify Data Types:** If your workflow tries to set a list state with a single value, or vice versa, Bubble will flag errors or behave oddly. Double-check that your state's data type matches the content you feed it.
- **Keep an Eye on Performance:** Most custom states won't slow your app because they're lightweight. But if you store hundreds of large

entries in a single list state, your page might lag. Consider more efficient data loading if you're dealing with massive sets of information.

DEBUGGING AND MAINTAINING CONTROL

When diagnosing issues with states—like an element not showing when you expect it to—Bubble's debug mode can be a lifesaver. I often enable debug mode, then walk through the workflows step by step. This way, I see the real-time value changes of each custom state on the page. If a state isn't being set correctly, or if a condition is referencing the wrong data, I'll spot it in the logs.

If things get especially complex, I sometimes create a small text box on-screen (visible only in debug or admin mode) that displays the current values of important states. This ephemeral debug panel helps me confirm at a glance which states are toggling on or off as I click around. Once I'm satisfied everything works, I simply hide or remove that text box from the final version.

THE FOUNDATION OF DYNAMIC EXPERIENCES

By now, you can probably see how custom states steer the dynamic side of Bubble. When combined with the platform's visual workflows and conditionals, states act like the signals that keep everything in sync. They let you craft advanced features—from multi-step forms to interactive dashboards—without constantly writing to the database or forcing page reloads. As soon as I embraced custom states, I found that even more ambitious UI ideas were within reach.

No matter what kind of project you're building—a social platform, a data dashboard, or an e-commerce site—chances are you'll rely on custom states somewhere along the line. They're one of Bubble's secrets to making experiences feel fluid and app-like. With states, your design can react to nuanced user behaviors in real time, delivering not just a website, but a living, interactive interface that users enjoy visiting again and again.

Chapter 14: Advanced Database Queries

When I reached the stage of working on more complex Bubble projects, I realized that the way I handle my database searches and data manipulation can drastically affect both the user experience and the performance of my app. I had become comfortable with the basics—like creating data types, defining fields, and performing simple searches—yet I soon realized there was a deeper level of expertise needed if I wanted to query large datasets with precision and speed. In this chapter, I'd like to delve into those more advanced strategies, including building powerful constraints, merging multiple searches, and even grouping results when you want to analyze data in aggregate. These tips will help you optimize your queries, reduce clutter, and give your users direct access to the insights they need.

THINKING BEYOND BASIC SEARCHES

Until I started tinkering with more complicated features, my go-to approach for filtering information in Bubble was to drag a repeating group onto a page and use "Do a search for…" with a few constraints. While that works fine in many situations—such as listing products by category or retrieving posts by published date—there's even more you can do behind the scenes.

For instance, you might need to display dynamic information based on multiple "OR" conditions, or you might want to combine two different search results to get a single list. When your data structure spans numerous related data types, you'll often tap into the more nuanced aspects of Bubble's query builder. By embracing these advanced techniques, you can avoid a messy pile of overlapping conditions or repeated workflows and keep your app both efficient and logically clean.

COMBINING CONSTRAINTS AND ADVANCED FILTERS

Any "Do a search for" block in Bubble lets you add multiple constraints that essentially mimic the "AND" logic—an item must meet all specified criteria. However, sometimes you don't want such rigid conditions. Let's say you want to pull a list of "Projects" that are either labeled as "High Priority" or "Urgent." One route is to run separate searches and then merge them. Alternatively, you can use advanced filters to build custom logic that checks item properties after the basic search completes.

I typically start by setting broad constraints in the initial query, like "Status is not empty," ensuring the data set is somewhat narrowed down at the database level. Then I use Bubble's ":filtered" method to refine it further using more sophisticated logic—like "This Project's tag contains 'High Priority' OR 'Urgent.'" Because ":filtered" works on the client side, it's not always the best for large volumes of data, but it's perfect if your initial search is already small. It gives you the flexibility to craft unique "OR" conditions, nested conditions, or even check multiple fields simultaneously.

MERGING MULTIPLE SEARCHES

One technique I often leverage is merging two separate searches into a single list. For instance, if I'm building a social platform, I might want to show both "Events I'm attending" and "Events recommended to me" in one feed. Neither a single "Do a search for" nor a single constraint fits this scenario perfectly because the logic is distinct for each set of records.

Here's how I do it:

- **First search:** "Upcoming Events where Current User is listed as an attendee."
- **Second search:** "Upcoming Events recommended to the Current User by friends."

Then I use Bubble's *merged with* operator to blend the two lists. Once merged, I might even apply a sort on the combined list, like sorting by date or popularity. This consolidated approach keeps the UI straightforward for users, while letting me handle the complexity in the background.

REFERENCING NESTED DATA TYPES

When you design your database, you often set up relationships among data types—for example, "Project" might link to a list of "Tasks," and each "Task" might reference a "Category." To search across these nested structures, you can chain references in your constraints. I remember a scenario where I wanted to find all projects that featured at least one task marked "Overdue." What I did was this:

Search for Projects where This Project's Tasks contains a Task whose 'Status' = Overdue.

Bubble's intuitive referencing system allows you to follow those links in your constraints. If your relationships are configured properly (for example, storing a list of tasks on the Project data type), you can build queries that effectively hunt through multiple layers seamlessly. In many coding environments, you'd have to manually join tables, but

Bubble's relational approach makes advanced queries like these more accessible.

GROUPING AND AGGREGATIONS

At some point, you may need to do more than just list entries. Perhaps you want an overall sum, average, or count. Bubble offers a "grouping" functionality that can be especially powerful for analytics-oriented dashboards or summary views. There's a "Group by" feature that lets me combine items based on a shared field—like grouping "Sales" entries by "Month." Then I can apply aggregations to each group:

- **Count:** Number of records in that group
- **Sum:** Total of a numeric field (e.g., total sales amount)
- **Average:** Mean value of a numeric field
- **Min/Max:** The smallest or largest value in that field

By using grouping, I can quickly display "Total Sales by Month" or "Number of Users by User Role" without writing separate queries for each role or month. It's a single query that organizes data around whichever dimension you choose. Then, I bind those grouped results to a repeating group or chart plugin, turning raw data into user-friendly summaries.

LEVERAGING :COUNT, :SUM, AND MORE IN EXPRESSIONS

Even outside of formal grouping, I regularly use expression-based aggregations in my search results. For example, a repeating group might have a data source of "Do a search for Orders," but inside a text element, I'll reference "Search for Orders:sum of total_amount" to show the combined revenue. Or maybe I'll do "Search for Items:count" to display how many items matched the query. In each scenario, these aggregator modifiers are your gateway to converting lists into meaningful statistics instantly. I've found they're especially handy for building dashboards where you want to show quick metrics without extra workflows.

BALANCING PERFORMANCE WITH LARGER DATASETS

As your data grows, advanced queries can place a heavier load on Bubble's servers—and potentially slow down your app if you're not careful. Here are a few ways I keep my searches snappy:

Performance Tip	Why It Helps

Limit the Initial Search Scope	Use constraints that reduce the dataset on the server side before applying advanced filters. The smaller the dataset, the faster the filter runs in the browser.
Index Key Fields	Define logical data structures (e.g., separate data types for repeated fields) and keep your queries referencing them. This approach often speeds up server-side searches.
Paginate Results	Instead of loading hundreds of records at once, show fewer items per page. Bubble's repeating group pagination helps reduce load times substantially.
Cache or Store Summaries	For frequently requested metrics or aggregates, consider saving the results in a dedicated data type or field, updating it periodically. This prevents repeated heavy calculations.

UTILIZING PRIVACY RULES WISELY

As a final note, advanced workflows can inadvertently reveal data to users if you're not managing privacy settings well. If your queries retrieve data from nested fields or external references, double-check that your privacy rules align with these new search paths. Bubble will restrict or hide fields that the user has no rights to view, so forgetting to set correct roles for nested object references can cause partial or broken search results. Conversely, you might accidentally give too much access if you skip setting the right constraints. Striking the right balance keeps your advanced searches secure and ensures legitimate users see precisely the data they need.

CULTIVATING A SEARCH-FRIENDLY MINDSET

Experience taught me that advanced queries are as much about good data modeling as they are about searching. If you map your relationships clearly—knowing where lists should live, how references flow, and which fields likely need indexing—your advanced queries will feel natural and run smoothly. It's worth taking the time to envision how users might want to slice and dice the data when you're structuring data types. That foresight goes a long way toward preventing slow performance or messy constraints down the line.

In the end, mastering advanced database queries in Bubble is both an art and a science. On one hand, you carefully orchestrate constraints, merges, and grouping to achieve the desired results; on the other, you monitor performance and remain vigilant about data security. Once you're comfortable with both sides of that equation, you'll see your application transform from a basic data display into a robust information hub—no matter how intricate your user needs become.

Chapter 15: Payment Integration and E-Commerce

Over the course of building Bubble applications, I've found that nothing feels quite as rewarding as deploying a functional online store or subscription-based service. There's a special thrill in seeing real transactions flow smoothly through your app, reflecting a solid union between product offerings, user trust, and secure payment processing. In this chapter, I'll guide you through the essentials of setting up payment gateways, creating a seamless checkout flow, managing orders, and ensuring your entire e-commerce experience feels both straightforward and secure.

WHY E-COMMERCE MATTERS IN BUBBLE

From my perspective, the power of Bubble's no-code platform comes into its own when you incorporate e-commerce features. Suddenly, your idea isn't just a neat web concept—it can become a revenue-generating venture. Whether you're selling digital downloads, physical goods, or subscription-based services, the flexibility that Bubble provides opens endless possibilities. Plus, Bubble makes it possible to integrate secure payment gateways with minimal fuss. That means you can focus more on your offerings and less on manual coding work.

ESTABLISHING PAYMENT GATEWAYS

Selecting the Right Provider: The first step I always take involves choosing a payment provider. Popular options like Stripe, PayPal, or Braintree each offer unique benefits and pricing structures. Think about your target audience (international buyers, recurring subscribers, etc.) and pick a gateway that resonates with your business model.

Setting Up Credentials: After choosing a provider, you'll generate API keys or client IDs that Bubble can use to authenticate transactions. In your Bubble Editor, you'll typically install or enable a relevant plugin. Once installed, the plugin's settings page prompts you for your test and live keys. I suggest experimenting in test mode first—this safe environment ensures you can try out the checkout process without actual funds changing hands.

Testing the Connection: Whenever I work on payment features, I confirm the connection is solid by doing a mock purchase. If your provider supports a "test card" number or sandbox mode, run an order through to confirm that the transaction logs show up on the provider's dashboard. Only then do I switch to live credentials.

BUILDING A PRODUCT CATALOG

In my experience, a tidy product catalog is central to any e-commerce site. You'll likely create a data type—let's call it **Product**—with fields like *name, price, description*, and *image*. For inventory tracking, consider adding an *inStock* quantity. Once set up, you can design a repeating group to showcase products in a clean, scrollable layout. At a glance, users can see item photos, names, and prices. I also like to include dynamic filters (like "category" or "price range") so customers can quickly find what interests them.

If you're offering digital goods—like an ebook or online course—adjust your fields to store relevant download links or membership access parameters. The flexibility you built into the **Product** data type can handle either physical or digital goods with just a few adjustments.

DESIGNING A CHECKOUT FLOW

Cart or Direct Purchase? For you, the choice might hinge on your business model. A multi-item shopping cart flow is typical for physical goods. However, if you sell single-use services (like a coaching session) or one-off downloads, a direct "Buy Now" option might be enough.

Adding Items to Cart: In a cart-based approach, I set up a **Cart** data type linked to the **User**, storing references to **Product** entries, plus quantity if needed. As someone navigates your app, I'll have "Add to Cart" buttons that create or update entries in the **Cart**. It's crucial to reflect changes in real-time so the user sees accurate totals or item counts.

Review and Payment: When the user is ready to check out, I redirect them to a "Review Order" page that shows the cart's contents, totals, and shipping details if applicable. The "Proceed to Payment" button triggers a workflow connecting to your payment provider's API. This step might include collecting card details (depending on your provider's security architecture) or redirecting to a secure hosted form. Bubble's integrations make each method remarkably simple: just choose the correct plugin action, fill in the order details, and let the provider handle card security.

Confirmation Page: On successful payment, I typically show a confirmation screen that includes an order summary and an email receipt. Keeping this consistent across your brand—same logo, style, and wording—helps to reinforce user trust, especially for first-time buyers.

MANAGING ORDERS AND STOCK

Order Records: Each completed transaction should generate an **Order** record in your database. Fields include the customer's **User** reference, a list of purchased products, total amount, shipping address (if needed), transaction ID from your payment provider, and an order status (*pending, shipped, delivered,* etc.). By storing these details, you can organize the order's lifecycle and quickly debug any customer inquiries or disputes.

Stock Synchronization: If you track inventory, decrement the *inStock* quantity for each product right after a successful payment. That helps avoid overselling if multiple users order the same product. I recommend a brief workflow step (run only when the payment is confirmed) to update the relevant product fields. And if your store is large, consider a backend workflow to systematically handle re-stocks or notify you when certain items run low.

Subscription Models: For those offering recurring services or memberships, an **Order** might represent a renewal cycle. Bubble can handle recurring billing by scheduling backend workflows that re-run payment requests at intervals. This automates membership updates, invoice generation, or usage-based billing. Just be sure to coordinate your provider's subscription APIs with Bubble's scheduling features carefully.

HANDLING REFUNDS AND DISPUTES

Real-world e-commerce occasionally means processing cancellations, returns, or disputes. When you handle refunds, the logic usually goes like this:

- **Locate the Transaction:** Use the *transaction ID* or *order ID* stored in Bubble to reference the purchase at your payment gateway.
- **Trigger the Refund Action:** Depending on your plugin, you might have a "Refund" or "Partial Refund" workflow step. You specify the amount to refund and confirm the reason code if needed.
- **Update Order Record:** Mark the **Order** as refunded or partially refunded. If stock items are being returned, you may want to increment *inStock* again or handle them through a separate returns process.

If a buyer disputes a charge externally (like through a credit card company), your payment provider usually notifies you through webhooks. You can set up backend workflows in Bubble to catch these notifications and update your **Order** records automatically. That way, you're never blindsided by a dispute or chargeback.

SECURITY CONSIDERATIONS

SSL Encryption: Always ensure your Bubble domain uses HTTPS (enabled by default on paid plans or custom domains). This encryption is foundational for safeguarding user information, especially on checkout pages where sensitive data is exchanged.

Offloading Card Details: In many cases, you'll want to redirect the actual card data handling to your payment provider, ensuring that you don't ever store raw card details in your Bubble database. Not only does this reduce your compliance burden, but it also makes user trust easier to maintain.

Privacy Rules: Double-check that your **Order** data is visible only to the rightful owners and your admin team. Payment logs, addresses, or other personal details shouldn't be accessible to unauthorized users. Bubble's data privacy tab can handle these restrictions effectively, but it's up to you to set them carefully.

TESTING YOUR COMMERCE WORKFLOWS

Before launching, I devote a session to methodically testing every step:

Test Scenario	Action Taken

Valid Payment	Use provider's test card numbers to ensure the checkout completes smoothly and that the new order is logged accurately.
Invalid Payment	Try an expired card to confirm your app shows a proper error message and blocks the transaction.
Cart Edits	Add multiple products, remove one, change quantities—verify that everything updates in real time and the total amount is correct.
Refund Flow	Initiate a refund from the admin panel and confirm the status updates properly in your Bubble app and payment provider's dashboard.

This careful test pass helps iron out any UI quirks, workflow missteps, or mismatched data that might surface after going live. I always make sure to test different price points, shipping choices, or coupon codes if available—anything that might stress-test my logic.

BUILDING FOR GROWTH AND SCALE

Optimizing Checkout Speed: A quick-loading checkout reduces cart abandonment. Minimizing large images and unnecessary data calls on your checkout page makes the user experience faster and less prone to frustration.

Promotions and Discounts: If you plan promotional codes or flash sales, consider how you'll store and validate them. You might create a **Coupon** data type with fields like *code*, *discount amount*, and *expiration date*. Then, when a user applies a code, your workflow adjusts the final price and logs which coupon was used.

Performance Under Load: Handling dozens or hundreds of orders simultaneously is a good problem to have, but it requires efficient data management. Using scheduled or backend workflows can distribute tasks like sending order confirmation emails or updating inventory, preventing your main user-facing pages from slowing down. If your store expands significantly, you might add scheduled crawls or batch updates that keep everything running smoothly.

FINAL THOUGHTS

Integrating payment processing and building an e-commerce ecosystem in Bubble isn't just about accepting credit cards; it's about creating a polished, trustworthy experience for your users. By carefully setting up gateways, designing a fluid checkout flow, managing inventory, and keeping a watchful eye on security, you're priming your app for real-world success. Every purchase, subscription, or donation becomes a sign that your Bubble app is delivering concrete value—something all of us as creators can celebrate. Embrace the challenge of e-commerce, refine your workflows, and you'll find that building a sustainable online business with Bubble is absolutely within your reach.

Chapter 16: Scheduling and Backend Workflows

WHY SCHEDULING WORKFLOWS MATTERS

One of the most transformative moments I had while deepening my Bubble skill set was when I realized that not every task in an application needs to happen right away. Sometimes, a process is better performed on a set schedule—like sending weekly newsletters, clearing old records, or running nightly maintenance routines. That's where Bubble's backend workflows and scheduling capabilities shine. Instead of tying up the user's browser or your app's front-end with lengthy calculations, you can shift those tasks to Bubble's back-end environment and set them to run anytime you want. This approach not only enhances performance but allows you to build more sophisticated applications with minimal effort.

INTRO TO BACKEND WORKFLOWS

Backend workflows in Bubble are like a behind-the-scenes engine that performs tasks without a user having to click a button or load a particular page. You access these workflows via the "Backend Workflows" tab in the Bubble Editor, and they're separate from the typical page-based workflow area. This separation is intentional: it ensures your normal user flows remain uncluttered while giving you a dedicated space to handle system-level operations. Whether you're organizing a file cleanup, generating reports, or automating a marketing campaign, these workflows let you schedule or trigger operations in the background, freeing up users to keep browsing without hiccups.

CREATING AND NAMING BACKEND WORKFLOWS

The process starts by creating a new backend workflow. After activating "Enable backend workflows" in your Settings, you'll see an option to create both "API Workflows" and "Recurring Events." Each type serves a unique purpose. API Workflows can be run on demand— either called from within your app's workflows, or from external apps if you've set up an external API endpoint. Recurring Events, on the other hand, do exactly what the name implies: they run repeatedly at set intervals, like once every day or every month.

When setting up a new backend workflow, give it a clear, descriptive name. It might be "nightly_data_cleanup" or "weekly_sales_digest." As someone who's maintained numerous Bubble apps, I've learned that naming clarity saves countless hours of confusion later on. Keep it direct so you know at a glance which workflow handles which process.

SCHEDULING WORKFLOWS: SINGLE EVENTS VS. RECURRING TASKS

Single scheduled events allow you to pick a specific time in the future for a workflow to run—like sending a reminder email 24 hours before an event starts. To set this up, you simply choose "Schedule API Workflow" from a normal workflow step in your app. Bubble then asks which backend workflow to run, along with the time you want it to fire. You can even pass data through, like the user's email or the event details, ensuring the process has the context it needs.

Recurring events are perfect for tasks that must repeat at regular intervals, such as generating a weekly report. Once you define the recurrence schedule, Bubble automatically triggers the workflow behind the scenes. In my projects, I rely heavily on recurring events for low-level housekeeping—like archiving old notifications every Sunday night. A single setup step handles it all, and I don't have to remember to press any buttons or manually run the script. It's a simple "set it and forget it" system.

PASSING DATA TO BACKEND WORKFLOWS

Scheduling and backend workflows become even more powerful when you can pass detailed data through them. Perhaps you're building a time-sensitive sales campaign: when a user enrolls, you might schedule a follow-up email three days later that references their name, purchase history, or a unique discount code. By configuring the workflow's parameter fields, I can feed all the necessary information into that future process. This practice gives me greater flexibility—each user can receive personalized notifications or follow-ups at just the right moment. All of that happens automatically, without requiring me to be awake at 3 a.m. to send a manual email.

BEST PRACTICES FOR COMPLEX SCHEDULING

In my experience, once you start building multiple scheduled events, it's crucial to stay organized. Whenever possible, I keep a dedicated list (even a simple spreadsheet) of which workflows exist, what triggers them, and when they run. This reference saves me from accidentally duplicating processes or forgetting why something's scheduled for Tuesday afternoons. For heavier apps with hundreds or thousands of users, it's also smart to consider potential conflicts—like too many large tasks firing simultaneously. Spreading out heavy jobs can prevent a backlog from bogging down performance.

I also love to add short "notes" inside each workflow step describing its purpose. Bubble's workflow interface supports a textual description, and it can be a lifesaver if you return months later to modify or debug something. A line like "This step sends a reminder email and logs the action in the audit table" instantly clarifies the step's intent.

MANAGING PERFORMANCE AND LOGS

Because backend tasks aren't visible on pages, debugging means checking logs. In the "Logs" section of the Bubble Editor, you'll see entries for each scheduled workflow run—whether it succeeded or hit an error. Whenever I test new scheduling features, I keep an eye on these logs to confirm everything fires when expected and that data flows correctly. If something doesn't run or completes too early, the logs usually provide a clue, like a missing field or a failed condition.

For performance, keep in mind that each scheduled workflow consumes server resources. If you schedule enormous data operations every minute, your app's responsiveness could suffer. As a rule of thumb, schedule resource-intensive tasks during lower-traffic windows, or break them into chunks using iteration or small offsets in time. Bubble's capacity-based model is generally forgiving, but a well-planned approach ensures your users never sense a slowdown.

EXAMPLE USE CASES

Overdue Reminders: Everyday, check which items are overdue in a project management app and send alerts. **Subscription Renewals:** Automatically charge customers monthly or yearly, with a workflow that updates renewal dates and transaction logs. **Data Cleanup:** Archive or delete entries that are older than a certain threshold, keeping your database lean. **Marketing Drips:** Schedule a series of emails that gradually roll out to new signups over the course of a week or month.

FINAL THOUGHTS

Scheduling and backend workflows bring your Bubble applications to a level that feels professional, automated, and robust. Instead of waiting for a user action, you can proactively manage tasks at precisely the right moment—whether it's seconds from now or months in the future. Mastering these capabilities opens doors to advanced features like automated billing, timely reminders, or data cleansing routines, all handled quietly behind the scenes. By embracing backend workflows, you not only streamline your user's front-end experience but also position your app for scalability, reliability, and growth. Once you get comfortable with these tools, you'll wonder how you ever built complex apps without them.

Chapter 17: Building Complex Repeating Groups

When I first discovered Bubble, the concept of a repeating group was a turning point in how I visualized dynamic data. A repeating group allows you to list items from your database—like orders, posts, or projects—and format them in a structured, repeatable pattern on the page. But there's much more potential here than just displaying a basic list. Over time, I learned how to harness repeating groups for more advanced layouts—incorporating nested data, calculations, dynamic filters, and even multiple data sources. In this chapter, I'll share the techniques I've picked up to build more sophisticated repeating groups that keep your app both functional and visually engaging.

RETHINKING THE BASICS

Long before you create a complex repeating group, it's helpful to confirm you're comfortable with the fundamentals. Typically, a repeating group has three key components:

- **Type of Content:** The data type each row or cell will display (e.g., "Product" or "User").

- **Data Source:** The "Do a search for…" condition or a custom state that feeds data into the list.
- **Cell Layout:** How each item is rendered in the cell—whether in a single column, multiple columns, or a grid.

Once you grasp the core flow—defining a type, linking the right data source, and laying out elements in each cell—you've got the building blocks for stronger applications. Complexities arise when you start nesting groups, adding calculations, or adjusting filters on the fly.

NESTED REPEATING GROUPS

One of my favorite techniques is to embed a repeating group within another repeating group. Imagine you're building a project management tool that lists projects in the outer repeating group and tasks in an inner repeating group. Each project cell might contain a smaller repeating group showing only the tasks belonging to that project. All you need to do is:

1. **Set the Outer Repeating Group:** "Type of Content" = Project, "Data Source" = Search for Projects.
2. **Add an Inner Repeating Group:** Inside the cell, "Type of Content" = Task, "Data Source" = Current cell's Project's List of Tasks.

Thanks to Bubble's relational database structure, that inner list can update in real time. This nesting approach is versatile, whether you're displaying comments under a post, product variants under a main listing, or user reviews aligned with each item. Just be mindful of performance—

every nested group queries additional data, so use it judiciously if you're dealing with large volumes.

ADVANCED FILTERING AND SORTING

With larger datasets, a simple "Do a search for…" might not cut it. You'll often need to let users slice, filter, or sort the results without refreshing the whole page. For instance, you might provide a dropdown to filter by category or a slider to adjust a price range. Here's how I approach it:

- **Set a Broad Data Source:** Use a minimal "Do a search for…" constraint to pull initial items. Example: "inStock = yes."
- **Use Conditionals or :filtered:** Rely on the repeating group's conditional logic or the ": filtered" operation to narrow results in real time. For example, "When user selects a category, filter the data accordingly."
- **Allow Sorting Options:** Sorting might be alphabetical, by price, or by a custom ranking algorithm. Bubble's "Sort by" feature makes it easy to rearrange items without reloading the entire page.

I often store a user's selected filters in custom states, so I can switch them instantly, avoiding extra writes to the database or lengthy refreshes. Combined with repeating groups, this creates a very fluid browsing or discovery experience, especially for e-commerce interfaces or dashboards.

CREATING MULTI-COLUMN, MULTI-ROW GRIDS

The default orientation for a repeating group is usually a vertical list, but you can turn it into a grid with multiple columns and rows. In the element's properties, you'll find a field for **Rows** and **Columns**. For a Pinterest-like layout or a product gallery, I usually set "Rows" to "Full List" (or an exact number) and "Columns" to 3 or 4, giving that classic grid appearance.

If you need truly dynamic grids—for example, different widths for certain columns under some conditions—consider using Bubble's new responsive engine. By placing a repeating group in a row-container or circle-container layout, you can also adapt how cells stack or wrap as the screen narrows. These fine-tuned controls help your app look professional on both widescreen desktops and small phones.

COMBINING MULTIPLE DATA SOURCES

Sometimes, you want a single repeating group to incorporate inputs from more than one place. For example, you might show upcoming events that a user is attending, merged with events recommended to them by friends (two separate searches). In Bubble, you can either:

- **Use "Merged with":** "Search for events where Attendees contains Current User" merged with "Search for events recommended to Current User."
- **Store in a Custom State:** Perform multiple searches, combine them in a list-type custom state, and set that list as the repeating group's data source.

Merging data sources can drastically simplify user interfaces, letting you present what appears to be a single feed while behind the scenes you're actually juggling multiple queries.

DYNAMICALLY CALCULATED COLUMNS

Every so often, I need a repeating group to display values that aren't explicitly in the database—like sub-totals, percentages, or counts of nested items. Let's say you have an "Order" repeating group, and you want each cell to show the combined price of its line items. You can achieve this by adding expressions inside text elements:

Current cell's Order's List of Line Items: sum of price

This approach retrieves the related "Line Items," sums up the price, and displays it instantly. It's a powerful technique for on-the-fly calculations. Just watch out for performance if your nested lists grow large. If calculations or queries become intensive, consider storing summary data (like total price) at the "Order" level and periodically updating it via workflows or backend routines.

CONDITIONAL FORMATTING AND INTERACTIVITY

Repeating groups become interactive when you apply conditional statements to highlight or show/hide elements based on data values. For instance, if a product's stock drops below a threshold, you could display a red alert icon within the repeating cell. Similarly, if a task is overdue, highlight its text or add a badge that says "OVERDUE."

I especially enjoy enabling users to click on a cell to reveal more info or drill down into a detailed view. A single repeating group cell can contain collapsible sections, conditional pop-ups, or triggers that set custom states. This transforms your repeating group into more than just a static list—it becomes a gateway for deeper data exploration.

PAGINATION AND "LAZY LOADING"

When your dataset is vast, loading all records can be inefficient. Bubble's repeating group properties let you select how many items to show per page. You can add page navigation controls—like "Next" and "Previous" buttons—to cycle through results. This not only improves performance but also keeps the layout clean.

Another option is "Vertical Scrolling," which loads items as you scroll. For example, I sometimes list posts in a social feed using this technique. As the user scrolls, more items appear, creating a continuous flow. Performance-wise, Bubble fetches the next batch in chunks, preventing the entire feed from downloading at once. It's a neat trick if you want an infinite-scroll experience.

DEBUGGING AND TESTING TIPS

Complex repeating groups can be tricky to perfect. Here are a few ways I've learned to troubleshoot:

Challenge	Solution
No Data Appearing	Double-check your data source. Ensure the user has permissions to see it, and verify any constraints or filters.
Slow Loading	Use fewer nested searches or implement pagination. Also, consider caching or storing computed fields to avoid repeated calculations.
Incorrect Sorting	Check that the field you're sorting on matches the data type (text vs. number vs. date). If the sort order looks

	reversed, flip the ascending/descending toggle.
Layout Misalignment	Margin, padding, or responsive settings can be off. Inspect each cell's layout to ensure they scale well for different devices.

FINAL THOUGHTS

Repeating groups are one of Bubble's signature features, but they can also be one of the most nuanced to master. By blending nested data, on-the-fly calculations, robust filtering, and interactive elements, your repeating groups can evolve into lively data explorers instead of simple lists. Whenever I'm aiming to showcase a large dataset in a captivating way, I reach for these advanced techniques: merging multiple sources, toggling detail views within cells, and bringing in powerful sorting and filtering.

Ultimately, a "complex" repeating group isn't just about complexity for its own sake— it's about making your data more immediately useful and meaningful to users. With thoughtful design and a knack for advanced search expressions, you'll soon discover that repeating groups are the heart of your app's user interface, empowering your audience to engage with data in a rich, intuitive style.

Chapter 18: Tips for Debugging and Troubleshooting

I remember the moment I realized what a lifesaver the right debugging strategies can be when building advanced features in Bubble. Getting stuck on an error message or a misfiring workflow can feel daunting, but the platform offers several built-in tools and best practices to help you spot issues quickly. In this chapter, I'll walk through the tactics I rely on to track down problems, refine my app's logic, and ensure that everything runs smoothly.

EMBRACING THE DEBUGGER

The Debugger is one of my go-to resources. When I'm testing, I add "?debug_mode=true" to my app's URL or hit the "Preview" in Debug Mode button in the editor. This triggers a special view that walks me step by step through each workflow, displaying what data is being manipulated and which conditions are firing. By pausing or moving slowly through each step, I can isolate exactly where an unexpected behavior starts. This clarity is invaluable: if I see that a condition never evaluates to true or that a data field isn't being updated, it pinpoints the crucial spot to fix. Without the Debugger, I'd be left guessing where the error begins.

LOGGING AND APP DATA INSPECTION

Beyond the Debugger, examining app logs helps me trace back a user's steps or confirm if a scheduled event actually triggered. In my experience, checking "Server Logs" from the Logs panel often reveals a clear explanation of workflow actions—like a database entry failure or a privacy rule blocking access. These logs detail timestamps, triggered workflows, and any errors that pop up. If something doesn't align with the user's reported issue, I'll note the discrepancy and investigate further. Inspecting the raw data in "App Data" can also be enlightening—I might discover a missing field value or identify data saved under the wrong conditions. Taking a few minutes to compare expected values against actual entries can unravel even the trickiest puzzle.

SYSTEMATIC TESTING OF WORKFLOWS

When a workflow behaves unpredictably, I adopt a systematic approach: break it down into smaller components and test each step individually. For instance, if I have a multi-step process that saves a record, updates a custom state, and then sends an email, I'll temporarily disable the last two steps and confirm that the first step works correctly. If it does, I'll reinstate the second step, then the third, watching carefully for the exact step that introduces the error. This incremental approach ensures I don't waste time rebuilding the entire process only to learn that the culprit was a tiny condition in step three.

REVIEWING CONDITIONS AND PRIVACY RULES

Another common source of confusion often lies in conditional statements or privacy settings. I once spent hours trying to figure out why a repeating group refused to display any data for certain users—only to realize I'd set up strict privacy rules that blocked one of the fields. A quick check in the Privacy panel confirmed restricted access for that user role, causing the list to appear empty. Now, whenever data goes missing, the first place I verify is the privacy tab. Similarly, if a conditional statement on a button doesn't trigger, I'll double-check the logic. Even small typos—like referencing the wrong custom state name—can halt an action.

TROUBLESHOOTING DESIGN AND RESPONSIVE ISSUES

Not all problems center on workflows. Sometimes layout quirks or responsiveness can throw off an otherwise functional app. If an element isn't displaying as expected, I'll open the responsive editor to watch how elements reposition at various screen widths. Often, a misaligned container or a group set to collapse incorrectly can cause hidden sections or overlapping text. I start by selecting the problematic element and checking its layout settings: is the minimum width too large? Are margins forcing it off the screen? By walking step by step through each breakpoint, I can track down the design glitch and shape a neater interface.

TESTING WITH DIFFERENT USER ROLES

Occasionally, an app works flawlessly for admin users but fails for regular members or guests. This mismatch usually arises from data visibility or workflow permissions. To steer clear of such pitfalls, I set aside a test account for each role. Logging in with these accounts helps me see exactly what they see. For example, if a VIP page doesn't load, I can confirm whether my role-based conditions are correct. It also validates that restricted content truly remains hidden from unauthorized users. Reproducing the issue under the same account type that the user has is an essential step for me, preventing role-based blind spots.

CLONING AND VERSION CONTROL

When I'm not sure how a major tweak will affect my existing features, I rely on Bubble's version control. I create a new development version—essentially a clone of my main app—so I can experiment freely without risking the live environment. If something breaks, I simply revert. Alternatively, if the fix works, merging those changes back into the main line is straightforward. This practice has saved me many times from rolling out half-tested solutions that accidentally break user experiences.

ISOLATING EXTERNAL INTEGRATIONS

If your app taps into external APIs or third-party plugins, debugging can get more involved. My strategy is to isolate the plugin or API call, testing it in a stripped-down environment or a separate page. By removing extraneous workflows, I confirm whether the integration itself is working properly. If a plugin call fails in its simplest form, the issue likely lies in the credentials or parameters. If it succeeds there but fails in my main app, the problem might be in how I'm handling the returned data or in a conflicting plugin. Narrowing the scope reduces guesswork and highlights the actual cause behind the malfunction.

KEEPING MEMOS ON RECURRENT ISSUES

After debugging an issue, I always jot down what went wrong and how I fixed it. It might sound tedious, but these notes turn into a treasure trove of lessons learned. Over time, patterns emerge—maybe I discover that each time I use a particular plugin, I have to adjust a default setting. By referencing previous notes, I can solve similar hiccups in minutes instead of brainstorming from scratch. These notes work best if they're concise—just a couple of lines capturing the core mistake and the resolution. Having that knowledge library keeps me proactive and bolsters my confidence when building new features.

STAYING CALM UNDER PRESSURE

It's easy to feel frustrated or fatigued when an app refuses to cooperate. Through experience, I've learned that a calm, methodical mindset is the best antidote to panic. Usually, I begin by reproducing the error consistently. If I can reliably trigger the bug, I have a clear window into what's happening. Next, I isolate each piece of the puzzle—workflow steps, custom states, conditional statements. By proceeding steadily and using the built-in tools, I nearly always spot something amiss, whether it's a data type mismatch or an overlooked privacy rule.

FINAL REFLECTIONS

Debugging in Bubble doesn't have to be stressful. With a combination of systematic testing, thorough log reviews, and the official Debugger, you can uncover most issues in far less time than guess-and-check approaches. By planning for possible pitfalls—checking user roles, validating privacy rules, confirming external integrations—you'll keep your development process smooth from start to finish.

Even the most advanced applications encounter snags, but knowing precisely how to tackle them forms the backbone of building reliable, user-friendly Bubble apps.

Chapter 19: Handling Version Control

When I began creating increasingly complex Bubble applications, one of the turning points in my development process was learning how to manage versions effectively. Having a solid version control strategy means you can keep experimenting and improving your app without worrying about breaking something irreparably. You can test new features, refine existing ones, and merge everything back together when it's polished and ready. In this chapter, I'll walk through how I approach version control in Bubble, offering a detailed look at each step and explaining why these tools are vital for building robust apps—especially if you have a team.

WHY VERSION CONTROL MATTERS IN BUBBLE

For me, version control in Bubble is both a safety net and a roadmap. It's a safety net because I can always roll back to an earlier state if a new feature introduces conflicts or bugs. It's also a roadmap, helping me keep track of the project's progression—every major update, every experiment, and every final tweak become documented milestones. If you're collaborating with others, version control keeps efforts organized and prevents you from stepping on each other's toes during development.

GETTING FAMILIAR WITH BUBBLE'S VERSIONING SYSTEM

Bubble provides built-in tools to create, manage, and merge different versions of your app. Out of the box, you get two primary workspaces:

- **Development Version:** This is your main sandbox, where you'll add new features, test changes, and refine logic before pushing it live.
- **Live Version:** Your production build, which real users interact with. It should represent the most stable, polished iteration of your application.

Beyond these two, you can create additional branches—sometimes called "working versions" or "feature branches"—to keep your experiments isolated. This is especially handy if you're working on a big feature that might disrupt the rest of the app while it's under development.

CREATING AND NAMING NEW VERSIONS

My process for creating a new version begins in the Bubble Editor's Version tab, where I click a button to generate a new branch. I give each branch a short but descriptive name—something like "feature-user-forum," "ui-revamp," or "billing-integration." This clear naming helps me remember what the branch contains at a glance. If other people are on the project, it makes collaboration much smoother, because they can see that "billing-integration" is where all the checkout improvements are happening.

DEVELOPING ON A PRIVATE BRANCH

Once I'm on a private branch, I'm free to experiment vigorously without worrying about disrupting the main flow of the app in Development. I might try new layouts, install and configure different plugins, or even restructure certain data types. If something goes wrong, I can revert changes in just that branch—or even discard the entire branch if the idea doesn't pan out. Being able to explore without affecting the main version keeps my mind at ease and fosters more creativity.

TESTING CHANGES THOROUGHLY

When I'm nearing completion of a feature, I test it thoroughly within that branch. Sometimes I invite collaborators to check it out as well, especially if we're working as a team. Each person can preview the private version by selecting it in the Version tab and generating a preview link. This field-testing in a controlled environment allows me to catch glaring issues before merging.

MERGING CHANGES BACK TO DEVELOPMENT

After everything looks good, I merge my branch into Development. Bubble's versioning interface compares both branches and shows any conflicts up front, though typically if I've been careful, conflicts are rare. The merge takes a snapshot of the private branch changes and applies them on top of Development. Right after merging, I do a quick pass in Development to ensure nothing unexpectedly broke. This final check is important because sometimes subtle differences in plugin settings or data structure can surface only after the merge is complete.

DEPLOYING TO LIVE

Once I'm satisfied with the updates in Development, I hit the "Deploy to Live" button, which pushes all changes to the production environment. From that moment on, real users see the updated interface and features. If an urgent fix or hot patch is needed, Bubble lets me make direct changes in Development and redeploy quickly. That agility is hugely beneficial if you discover post-launch bugs or critical issues you want to address immediately.

ROLLING BACK WHEN NEEDED

On occasion, I've introduced changes that caused unexpected glitches. In times like these, the ability to revert to a specific deployment can be a lifesaver. Bubble logs each deployment, letting me pick a past version to restore. Within seconds, my Live environment reverts to that stable snapshot. Of course, data changes made by real users in the meantime remain in the database—rolling back only affects the app's structure and workflows, not the user-generated content stored in the database.

COLLABORATING WITH A TEAM

When multiple developers or designers are involved in a Bubble project, version control becomes a collaborative hub. We create separate branches for each ongoing feature, so everyone can work in parallel without overriding each other's work. Communication is key: we name branches consistently, schedule merges at times that are convenient for the group, and update each other about potential conflicts (like a heavily refactored workflow or a drastically redesigned page). By syncing often and merging responsibly, we keep the main Development version fresh and avoid complicated conflict resolution later.

HELPFUL TIPS AND BEST PRACTICES

- **Keep Branches Short-Lived:** Resist letting big feature branches linger for weeks without merging. The longer a branch stays isolated, the more likely it'll be out of sync with Development, which can create merge headaches.
- **Use Descriptive Commit Messages:** Although Bubble's commits aren't quite like traditional git commits, adding clear notes or change descriptions whenever you merge helps track why you moved forward.
- **Maintain a Regular Merge Schedule:** If you have multiple collaborators, plan on merging frequently—every few days or weekly—so changes don't pile up.
- **Be Mindful of Database Schema Edits:** Significant changes to data types can create friction when merging. Document these alterations so that merging branches that rely on the old schema doesn't break things.

CONFIDENCE IN CONTINUOUS IMPROVEMENT

Before I fully embraced Bubble's version control, I often worried I'd break my entire application with an ambitious new feature. That fear sometimes stifled experimentation. Adopting a structured versioning habit removed those barriers. Now, I'm comfortable trying out bold ideas, knowing I can always revert. And if a feature works, merging it back is straightforward. This loop of "branch, create, test, merge, deploy" has made my development cycles more efficient, predictable, and fun.

Overall, handling version control in Bubble is less about memorizing elaborate commands and more about adopting a logical workflow that involves branching, testing, merging, and smoothly deploying updates. Following these steps frees you to push forward with new ideas, confident that you can roll back if needed. And once your project grows large—or your team does—solid version control practices transform from a nice extra into a fundamental necessity for maintaining a stable, evolving application.

Chapter 20: Performance Optimization Techniques

When I first started experimenting with more advanced apps in Bubble, I quickly realized that no matter how visually polished or feature-rich my projects became, performance was key to a great user experience. If pages took too long to load or workflows lagged behind user actions, it didn't matter how compelling my design was. Over time, I learned to fine-tune each part of the Bubble ecosystem to make my apps feel as snappy and seamless as possible. In this chapter, I'll share my favorite performance optimization techniques—from structuring data efficiently to managing workflow complexity—so you can keep your own apps responsive at scale.

UNDERSTANDING BUBBLE'S CAPACITY

It's important to remember that Bubble uses a **capacity-based model** for server resources. This setup means your app's ability to handle concurrent workflows, database operations, and user interactions depends on how much capacity your plan provides. When your app scales up and more users or background processes are active at once, you may see slowdowns if you exceed your capacity. To manage this risk, I keep an eye on the *Logs* tab in the Bubble Editor, checking for capacity spikes or repeated warnings about exceeding limits. If your product is popular enough to push beyond those limits, consider upgrading or optimizing the underlying workflows so they consume fewer resources.

BUILDING AN EFFICIENT DATABASE SCHEMA

The architecture of your database is the backbone of performance. Whenever I design a data structure, I aim to avoid unnecessary complexity. For instance, if I notice that a particular data type has too many fields—especially if some aren't used often—consider splitting them into a related data type. Large text fields or images in your main records can slow down searches, so I keep them in a separate type or store them as files.

I've also found it crucial to minimize how often I write or update data. When your workflows update many fields in one go, Bubble synchronizes all those changes and can briefly stall if the database is large. If possible, combine related information in fewer write operations, or schedule some updates later in a backend workflow. By refining your schema and storing only what you need, your app will query data faster and handle more users simultaneously.

APPLYING STRATEGIC SEARCH AND FILTERING TECHNIQUES

One common performance bottleneck arises when you're pulling large volumes of data unnecessarily. If a repeating group or chart loads thousands of records when the user only needs to see the first 20, it can lead to slow page loads. I address this by:

- **Using Constraints:** In "Do a search for...," limit results on the server side. For example, only show items created today, or cap the returned list at a certain number.
- **Partial Loading:** For lists that may grow large, enable "Vertical scrolling" or "Ext. vertical scrolling" so elements render only when needed, preserving resources.
- **Conditional Filters:** If you must apply heavier filters—like complex "OR" logic—try to narrow down the dataset first with simpler constraints before applying advanced filters in the browser.

These measures let you serve just the right amount of data at the right time, boosting responsiveness significantly.

OPTIMIZING WORKFLOWS

I compare a workflow to a script that needs to run behind the scenes—if it's too lengthy or triggers multiple downstream processes, it can hog resources and delay other user actions. Here's how I refine workflows to keep them lean:

1. **Combine Steps Wisely:** When possible, merge related actions into a single step using "Make changes to a thing" or "Create a new thing." Fewer steps mean fewer round-trip operations to the server.
2. **Check Conditions Early:** If an action should only happen under specific conditions, use "Only when…" to skip the entire step if it's not needed. This approach prevents wasteful database writes or unneeded calculations.
3. **Leverage Backend Workflows:** Any task that isn't immediately visible to the user—batch data operations, sending follow-up emails, etc.—can often be offloaded to a scheduled or recurring backend workflow. Doing so frees up the front end to respond faster.

LAZY LOADING AND CACHING

In some scenarios, your app will refer to the same data multiple times—like user details or product lists. Rather than fetching them fresh each time, consider caching or storing that data in a custom state on page load. For example, if the user navigates through multiple tabs but still needs the same set of product information, you can load it once, store it in a **list-type custom state**, and reference that state repeatedly. Just be cautious with very large lists, as storing thousands of items in a state can eat up the browser's memory. A balance between caching frequently used data and not overloading the client is where I've found the sweet spot.

RESPONSIVE DESIGN AND PERFORMANCE

Sometimes a page layout that looks terrific might still be resource-heavy. If you embed massive images, complex repeating group structures, or numerous conditional elements, the browser must do extra work rendering it all. My rule of thumb is to scale images sensibly—size them outside of Bubble before uploading—and keep only the necessary visual elements on initial load. I also break up very dense pages into multiple tabs or subpages if they become unwieldy. This approach reduces the initial loading time while still allowing advanced users to dive into deeper content on demand.

MONITORING LOGS AND CPU USAGE

Throughout an app's life cycle, monitoring your performance metrics is vital. I routinely check the **Logs** to see if certain workflows spike capacity usage or if there's an unexpected traffic pattern. Bubble displays metrics such as CPU usage and which requests consume the most resources. If I see a particularly heavy workflow appear often, that's my cue to investigate—maybe break it into smaller tasks or schedule it during low-traffic times. Monitoring these details regularly can prevent small inefficiencies from spiraling into full-blown performance bottlenecks.

USING PRIVACY RULES FOR EFFICIENCY

Privacy rules don't just protect data—they also influence performance by filtering records server-side. By granting users access only to the data they should see, Bubble preemptively prunes results before sending them to the client. This can cut down how much data transmits over the network, lightening the load on the user's browser. For example, I've created roles that can only see certain types of objects or fields, so the "Search" requests omit everything else. These rules effectively become additional constraints, helping your app stay lean while upholding security.

LOAD BALANCING WITH BACKEND SCHEDULES

If your application manages resource-intensive tasks—like analyzing thousands of rows or generating repeated notifications—running them all at once can degrade performance for everyone else. I often distribute these processes over time using **backend workflow scheduling**. Instead of handling a large batch in a single shot, schedule smaller chunks at staggered intervals ("Process 100 records every two minutes"). This manual load balancing ensures the system stays responsive, especially if you hover near your capacity limit. You can further optimize by placing tasks during off-peak hours when overall user traffic is low.

SCALING PLANS AND ADDITIONAL CAPACITY

If your project grows popular enough—and you've optimized your data, workflows, and design thoroughly—there might come a time when you hit the upper bound of your Bubble plan's capacity. In these situations, consider scaling up by adding capacity units or upgrading your plan. While it's tempting to jump to a higher tier, I personally do a final check on whether there's more optimization left on the table. Often, refining a few heavy workflows can buy you more runway before incurring higher monthly costs.

FINAL THOUGHTS

Performance optimization in Bubble is an ongoing process. Each time you add features, shift designs, or see a surge in traffic, you'll want to reassess your data structure, workflow strategies, and server usage. I've found that even small changes—a reduced search constraint or a switch to lazy loading—can dramatically improve page load times and user satisfaction. By leaning on Bubble's built-in monitoring tools, refining your data access patterns, and minimizing the overhead of each workflow, I've consistently maintained apps that run quickly and scale with user demand.

Use these techniques as both a foundation and a continual checklist. When you methodically optimize at every layer—from database schema to front-end UI—the result is a nimble application that keeps users engaged. After all, there's no better feeling than seeing your creations run as smoothly in peak traffic as they do in your personal test environment—just as you'd envisioned.

Chapter 21: Deploying Your Bubble App

PREPARING FOR LAUNCH

When I first built an application that felt ready for the world, I remember feeling both excited and apprehensive about "going live." Sure, it was thrilling to imagine real users interacting with what I'd created, but questions kept popping up: Is the database configured properly? Will new sign-ups flow smoothly? This chapter aims to put those nerves at ease by walking you through the key steps and considerations for deploying your Bubble app. There's a lot to cover—domain setup, version checks, post-launch monitoring—but getting these right can mean a cleaner, quicker launch that resonates positively with users from day one.

CHOOSING BETWEEN FREE AND PAID PLANS

Bubble offers multiple plan tiers, each with different capacities and features. If your app is relatively small and you're comfortable with the Bubble subdomain (like "myapp.bubbleapps.io"), you can deploy on the free plan. That said, if your audience is growing or you want to use a custom domain, you'll probably opt for a paid plan. In my experience, upgrading often unlocks beneficial perks—like increased capacity, reduced Bubble branding, and better performance under heavier loads. I usually weigh the cost against the app's goals. If I'm testing a small idea, the free tier might be enough, but once I see traction, the paid tiers make a huge difference in delivering a polished experience.

SETTING UP A CUSTOM DOMAIN

For those ready to present a professional image, connecting a custom domain is often a must. I begin by purchasing a domain through a registrar—popular choices include GoDaddy, Namecheap, or Google Domains. After that, I head into Bubble's Settings tab to configure this domain. Bubble will provide two CNAME records (or A records, depending on the approach) to enter within your registrar's DNS settings. Once these records propagate—usually within a few minutes to a few hours—switching your app to that custom URL is as easy as selecting it in the Bubble Editor.

From my viewpoint, having a clean, branded URL is a game-changer for user trust. The moment they see "www.myapp.com" instead of a bubbleapps.io link, it immediately feels more legit. Just make sure to coordinate your name servers and DNS updates carefully to avoid downtime or misconfiguration.

FINALIZING THE DEVELOPMENT PROCESS

Before hitting that "Deploy" button, I take a step back and confirm everything is where it should be. I'll run through these quick checks:

- **Design Consistency:** Scan through each page for mismatched styles, placeholder text, or uneven margins.
- **Workflow Validation:** Use the Bubble Debugger or logs to ensure major workflows—like sign-ups, payments, or data creation—execute as intended.
- **Data Privacy and Roles:** Confirm that sensitive data is hidden from public view and that the right users can see the right records.
- **Performance Check:** Quickly test crucial pages for load speed. If anything lags, consider short-term optimizations—like limiting displayed data or compressing large images—before launch.

This mini audit is especially useful if your app has grown organically. It ensures you're not leaving behind half-finished pages or dev-only placeholders that might confuse new visitors.

PUSHING FROM DEVELOPMENT TO LIVE

Bubble's version control system keeps your development environment separate from your live environment. When everything looks good in Development, I open the Version tab and select "Deploy Development to Live." At this moment, Bubble merges your final changes to the live version, usually within seconds. I'll then visit the live URL and quickly click around to confirm nothing broke in transit. If any immediate issues pop up—like missing data or unexpected errors—I revert or make quick fixes in Development and re-deploy. This iterative approach has saved me countless times from letting a bug linger in front of real users.

HANDLING POST-LAUNCH TASKS

Going live isn't the end of your journey. Rather, it's a transition into the next phase: real-world usage. Here's what I focus on once the site is public:

- **Monitoring Logs:** For at least the first few days, I'll keep the Bubble Logs tab open periodically to watch for errors, capacity overages, or suspicious activity.

- **User Feedback:** Whether you embed a feedback widget or rely on emails, gather user impressions so you can quickly address confusion or friction in the user experience.
- **Analytics Integration:** If measuring user behavior is essential, I'll set up Google Analytics or another service. Bubble's plugin ecosystem also has metrics tools you can embed directly in your pages.

I see these steps as my real-time barometer of app health. If I spot spikes in errors or feedback about slow load times, I jump back into Development, make adjustments, and deploy fresh fixes.

SWITCHING AND MANAGING VERSIONS

Once the app is live, I keep iterating. But to avoid disruptions, I do so in Development in parallel. Let's say I'm introducing a big new feature—like a new dashboard. I'll build and test it in Development or a separate branch. When I'm ready, I merge it into Development, give it a final pass, and then push it to Live. This continuous cycle of safe changes means the live user base only sees stable, tested updates, preserving their trust in the platform's reliability.

ENSURING A SCALABLE FOUNDATION

If you anticipate an influx of users—maybe a marketing campaign or a public release—it's wise to consider how your Bubble app will handle the traffic. Bubble automatically scales to an extent, but each plan has capacity limits. If you expect hundreds or thousands of concurrent users, I plan readiness by:

- **Upgrading Capacity:** Subscribing to a plan with more server units helps handle bursts of concurrent usage.
- **Using Backend Workflows:** Offloading heavy processes to scheduled events or data API endpoints to keep front-end interactions smooth.
- **Pre-launch Testing:** Running load tests (or inviting a Beta pool of users) to identify slow queries or minor bottlenecks. Fixing them before a mass audience arrives saves headaches later.

CUSTOM DOMAINS, SSL, AND SECURITY

If you're gathering personal information or accepting payments, securing your site with SSL is non-negotiable. Bubble typically offers SSL for custom domains on paid plans. You'll note a little lock icon in the browser once it's properly set up—signaling a secure connection. In my opinion, enabling that lock does more than just protect data in transit; it also reassures users that your app is trustworthy and professional.

While you're in the security mindset, double-check privacy rules and user roles. Are admin pages locked down? Do only certain roles have access to sensitive data types? Tying up these loose ends around deployment prevents embarrassing oversights once the app is publicly visible.

POST-DEPLOYMENT MONITORING AND UPDATES

Launching your Bubble app is like opening the doors to a new storefront: traffic flows in, but the real work is ongoing. I keep tabs on user sign-ups, usage patterns, and any unexpected behavior through plugins or external analytics tools. With actual data at hand—like which pages get the most visits or which features users skip—I can refine the user experience more effectively.

Don't worry if you spot small issues or get suggestions immediately after deploying. Iterative improvement is a strength of Bubble's approach. Refine the design or fix logic in Development, deploy quickly, and your audience sees the update in real time. Over time, these small continuous improvements amount to a robust, finely tuned product.

FINAL THOUGHTS

Deploying your app is both a technical step and a milestone in your creative journey. All the prototyping, workflow building, and design choices come together in a single moment when you decide you're ready for an audience. Make no mistake: it's a huge achievement. But it's also the start of a new chapter—listening to user feedback, scaling gracefully, and keeping your software fresh.

I've come to love how Bubble streamlines the process, reducing the typical headaches of uploading code to servers or fretting about hosting configurations. Instead, I can focus on shaping the best possible experience for my audience. So when you're ready to hit that "Deploy to Live" button, take a breath, savor the excitement, and step confidently into the next phase of your Bubble journey.

Chapter 22: Integrating User Profiles and Social Logins

WHY USER PROFILES ARE ESSENTIAL

One of the most exciting parts of building any application is giving users the sense that the space belongs to them. In my experience, that feeling starts with user profiles. These profiles are more than just a username and photo; they help people express who they are, store personal information, and connect meaningfully with each other. If you're aiming for greater engagement or more personalized interactions in your app, a well-crafted user profile section is often the way to go. In this chapter, I'll walk through setting up profiles, uploading images, managing extra fields, and integrating social logins to simplify the sign-in process.

STRUCTURING YOUR USER DATA

To begin, I like to think carefully about what kind of details I want each user to store. Beyond an email and password, you might include fields like:

- **Username or Display Name:** This can be shown publicly, especially in social or community-based apps.
- **Profile Picture:** An image field adds a personal touch and helps users recognize each other's accounts.
- **Bio or Status:** Let people share a short description about themselves or their interests.
- **Location:** If location-based features matter—like events nearby—storing the user's city or coordinates can come in handy.
- **Roles or Permissions:** Maybe you want to differentiate admins, premium subscribers, or any other tier. This is typically managed with yes/no or text fields.

In Bubble, the "User" data type is built-in, so you already have an email field and password security structure. I find it easiest to add extra fields under this "User" type. That way, each user record consolidates essential information in one place, making it simpler to reference user-specific data throughout the app.

DESIGNING A PROFILE PAGE

Next comes the fun part—showcasing user information on a dedicated profile page. In my own layouts, I like to feature a header with the user's display name and profile picture, followed by sections for bio, location, or social links. Here's the basic setup:

1. **Create a Profile Page:** In the Bubble Editor, add a new page named something like "Profile," with a data type of "User" if you plan on sending user-specific information.
2. **Add User Elements:** Insert text elements for the display name, an image element for the profile picture, and any other fields you want to highlight. Make them dynamic by referencing "Current Page User's [field]."
3. **Enable Editing (If Needed):** Some apps let people edit their profiles. You might put an "Edit" button that navigates to a form for updating user details. Once the user clicks "Save," it adjusts their account in the database.

By default, Bubble ensures each user can only edit their own data (unless you've granted broader permissions). This means your profile page remains secure while still being highly customizable. And if you want to display other users' profiles, simply pass their user record to the page in a workflow. Bubble's dynamic data references ensure the correct profile details fill in automatically.

PHOTO UPLOADS AND FILE HANDLING

One of the first changes I make when building a profile system is to allow users to upload or change their profile picture. I typically insert a picture uploader element alongside an image element already showing their current photo. The workflow goes like this:

- **When the user uploads an image:** Save that image to their "profilePicture" field in the database.
- **Auto-update display:** The profile page's image element is set to "Current User's profilePicture." As soon as the database updates, the image refreshes in real time.
- **Optional Crop or Resize:** If you want standard dimensions, you can integrate a plugin that crops or resizes images at upload.

Generally, Bubble handles file storage in its own Amazon S3 bucket, so you don't have to configure any external hosting. Just keep an eye on your app's plan limits if your users upload many high-resolution images; you might up your plan or compress those images for better performance.

INTRODUCING SOCIAL LOGINS

Social logins, such as signing in with Google or Facebook, simplify onboarding drastically. Users skip the tedious "create password" step and can jump directly into your app. In my experience, providing these options often boosts registration rates, especially on mobile devices where people may prefer not to type lengthy details on small keyboards. Bubble supports social logins primarily via plugins:

- **Google:** The Bubble plugin helps you configure a Google app in your Google Cloud console. Once set, you get a client ID and secret, which you paste into Bubble's plugin settings.
- **Facebook:** Similarly, you create a Facebook developer app, retrieve your keys, and enter them in Bubble's plugin for Facebook OAuth.
- **Others:** Twitter, LinkedIn, or Microsoft can also be integrated. These usually require custom or third-party plugins if they aren't provided in Bubble's default plugin library.

After installing and configuring your chosen plugin, you'll add a "Sign up with X" button or workflow action. When clicked, Bubble redirects the user to that platform's OAuth screen. Upon successful authentication, the user is logged in and a new account is created if needed. I love how streamlined it is—I don't have to store external passwords or manage tokens. Bubble orchestrates the heavy lifting behind the scenes.

MAPPING USER DATA FROM SOCIAL PLATFORMS

Beyond authentication, social logins often provide basic user data like name, profile picture, or email. Bubble can retrieve these details automatically, populating the user record in the database. Here's the approach I take:

1. **Check Plugin Fields:** In the plugin's configuration page, see what user attributes are available (e.g., "Current user's Google profile image").
2. **Save to Database:** As soon as the user logs in via the workflow, I might add a step "Make changes to Current User" and map each social field to the corresponding user fields. For instance, "profilePicture = Current user's Google profile image."
3. **Handle Missing Data:** Sometimes a social platform doesn't share certain user details. In those cases, I set a condition so that if the data is blank, the user fields remain unchanged or revert to placeholders.

This quick synchronization ensures newly registered accounts have the essential user info they need. It also means first-time logins feel more personalized—like seeing your profile picture instantly appear in the app.

SECURITY AND PERMISSIONS

Whenever user data is involved, I make sure to configure privacy rules. For instance, restrict who can view or edit private profile fields—like an email address or phone number. In Bubble's data privacy tab, you might specify: "Only Current User can see their email" or "Friends can see each other's phone fields." By storing user role or subscription data in the "User" record, you can also shape conditionals around permissions—like whether a user is allowed to view certain pages or manage certain admin tasks.

And don't forget to keep login channels consistent. If you offer both traditional and social login, be sure the user can still access their account even if they switch from Google to email one day. Often, I store the same "User" record if the email matches, ensuring no duplicate accounts. If a conflict arises, I guide them to merge or choose a single sign-in method to avoid confusion down the road.

MAKING PROFILES DISCOVERABLE (IF DESIRED)

Whether or not you want user profiles to be visible to others depends on your app's nature. If it's a collaborative platform or a social network, discoverability might be crucial. In that scenario, I might create a user directory with a repeating group listing all active users. Tapping on a username navigates to their profile page. For privacy, I only display fields the user has chosen to share publicly. This combination of a user list plus individual profile pages can spark engagement within your community, especially if you allow comments, follow features, or message threads connected to each profile.

ENCOURAGING PROFILE COMPLETENESS

A common technique to enhance the experience is prompting new sign-ups to fill out more details. For instance, after their first login, display a short "Complete Your Profile" wizard or progress bar tracking how many fields they've provided (photo, bio, location, etc.). This small nudge can help your users feel invested and make them aware of features they might otherwise skip. And if certain profile elements—like a phone number—are critical for your app, you can mark them as mandatory or block access to certain features until they're provided.

PRACTICAL MAINTENANCE TIPS

Data Cleanup: If you see incomplete or abandoned profiles, consider removing them or marking them for follow-up with an email prompt. **Profile Updates & Reminders:** Set up a recurring workflow to remind users to refresh their details if they haven't updated them in a long while. **Photo Moderation (If Needed):** For user-uploaded images, you might integrate a moderation service or request that individuals comply with guidelines.

FINAL REFLECTIONS

Integrating user profiles and social logins not only makes your application feel more personal but also streamlines the entire onboarding journey. With just a few clicks, newcomers can sign up via trusted platforms like Google or Facebook, and then refine their profile details in-app. Meanwhile, existing users can personalize their experience, uploading photos, bios, and connecting with others. For me, it's one of those features that instantly upgrades an app from "interesting idea" to a living, breathing community space.

By defining the fields, designing profile pages, and leveraging social login workflows, you'll be well on your way to delivering a more engaging, user-friendly environment. Once people see their own faces, names, and interests reflected back at them, they tend to stick around longer and return more often—giving you the perfect foundation for growth and long-term success.

Chapter 23: SEO and Marketing Tools

MY JOURNEY INTO BUBBLE SEO

When I first started building apps on Bubble, I quickly realized that creating a visually appealing application was only half the battle. If search engines and potential users couldn't find my app, none of those design flourishes mattered. That's where an understanding of **SEO (Search Engine Optimization)** and marketing tools becomes invaluable. Over time, I've learned how Bubble provides just enough features to help you optimize your app for search engines, plus ways to track—and increase—traffic using various marketing strategies. In this chapter, I'll share the most helpful SEO techniques and marketing tactics I've discovered, so your Bubble app can attract the audience it deserves.

OPTIMIZING META TAGS AND DESCRIPTIONS

One of the first things I tackled in my SEO journey was **meta tags**. Bubble makes it fairly straightforward to set titles, descriptions, and keywords for each page you build. From the "SEO / metatags" tab in your app's **Settings**, I can define default meta descriptions that appear across the website, plus individual tags per page. In my experience, a well-structured title tag and a compelling description help search engines understand what each page is about and encourage users to click when they see your site in search results.

Whenever I have multiple pages that serve unique purposes—like a "Landing" page or a "Blog Post" page—I customize their meta titles and descriptions carefully. That includes highlighting relevant keywords early in the title, and ensuring the description is concise yet descriptive. A strategic approach to meta tags not only boosts discoverability but also enhances the first impression potential visitors get in their search listings.

CHOOSING FRIENDLY URLS

In traditional coding environments, modifying URL slugs often requires complex routing rules. By contrast, Bubble allows me to designate page paths manually, so I can decide whether a page should be accessible at something like *mysitename.com/register* or *mysitename.com/?page=123*.

I've found that **human-readable URLs**—short strings containing real words—are both more user-friendly and better for SEO. They reassure visitors that the link leads to a real, relevant place without random strings of letters and numbers.

When building dynamic pages (such as a blog article), I set up a *slug* for each entry in my database. Bubble easily pulls that slug into the URL structure, creating a direct path like *mysitename.com/post/my-article-title*. This structure signals search engines that the page is about "my article title," improving how well it may rank for that phrase.

MOBILE RESPONSIVENESS FOR BETTER SEO

It's no secret that Google and other search engines reward sites that cater to mobile users. Given how many people browse on phones or tablets, **mobile responsiveness** has a huge impact on page ranking. Bubble's responsive editor helps ensure each page scales correctly, but I also pay attention to load times on slower connections. Compressing images, limiting large animations on mobile views, and using minimal repeating group data can go a long way toward improving my app's performance—an important factor in Google's assessment of mobile-friendly sites.

I usually test my app using both a phone and a low-bandwidth simulator to see if pages load within a reasonable time. If anything seems sluggish, I refine the layout or offload certain data until visitors really need it. This approach ensures new users aren't instantly turned off by slow performance, and it keeps me on good terms with search engine algorithms.

STRUCTURED DATA AND SOCIAL SHARING

While not mandatory for every project, the use of **structured data** can be a boon if you're building something like a recipes or events directory. You can embed special markup (like schema.org tags) to help search engines parse information more accurately. Bubble doesn't have an out-of-the-box interface for structured data, but I've inserted small code snippets in the "Page HTML header" section for advanced SEO. For me, it took a bit of trial and error—using the "HTML Element" or editing the "Head" area—but once set up, search engines like Google can display your results with richer previews, including images or star ratings.

Additionally, for social **sharing features**, I configure *Open Graph* tags in the SEO settings. These tags define the thumbnail, title, and description that appear when someone shares your link on platforms like Facebook or Twitter. A well-chosen thumbnail can be the difference between someone clicking through or scrolling past, so I pick images that quickly convey the app's value or theme.

USING MARKETING PLUGINS AND INTEGRATIONS

Beyond the SEO basics, Bubble's plugin ecosystem helps me extend my marketing reach. Need an **email marketing** solution? You can install plugins for Mailchimp or other major providers, syncing user sign-ups or newsletter subscriptions seamlessly. Likewise, if you want to track ad conversions from Google Ads or Facebook, there are dedicated plugins to add tracking pixels directly on your pages. This step is crucial if you run paid campaigns and want to gauge ROI accurately.

I also like to integrate with **Google Analytics**, which I do by dropping a tracking snippet in the SEO settings or by using a plugin. That way, I see real-time data about who's visiting, which pages get the most attention, and how long people stay. Over time, these insights shape my marketing strategies, spotlighting areas for improvement or features worth promoting further.

HANDY TECHNIQUES FOR LEAD GENERATION

Once your SEO has done its job of driving organic traffic, you want a way to capture leads or potential customers. Bubble's drag-and-drop forms let me create **email capture** or **contact us** sections within minutes. I often add a pop-up or a header bar inviting users to subscribe for updates or special offers. When they do, the email funnels into a data type or an external email provider, so I can follow up. Even a simple sign-up prompt can go a long way toward building a mailing list or potential client database.

If you're offering a free resource—like an eBook or a product demo—don't forget to track conversions. Setting a workflow step to increment a "downloads" field each time someone gets your resource provides clarity on which lead magnets work best. With that metric, you can optimize your landing page or pivot your marketing copy accordingly.

RUNNING AND TRACKING CAMPAIGNS

For times when I run **paid ad campaigns**, whether on Google, Facebook, or LinkedIn, I tie the tracking into my Bubble app to measure conversions. Typically, each ad platform gives me a JavaScript snippet (a pixel or a tag), which I paste into the page's header or install via a plugin. Then, after a user signs up or makes a purchase, I trigger the snippet to log that event. Seeing these conversions in the ad dashboard helps me judge which keywords or audience segments yield the best ROI, so I can fine-tune my budget or messaging.

For email campaigns, I rely on integrated services that let me build follow-up sequences. Nearly every time I do a mass email, I link back to a specific landing page with a unique URL parameter. That parameter helps me identify which campaign the click came from, so I can separate results and see if the subject line or timing was effective.

Over a few tests, patterns often emerge, making it easier to refine future campaigns.

TIPS FOR CONTINUOUS IMPROVEMENT

The beauty of marketing and SEO is that it's never a one-and-done process. Every time I implement a new approach—like adjusting a headline or creating a fresh blog post—I'll measure the outcome. If a tweak to my meta description raises click-through rates, I keep it. If a new ad set falls flat, I pivot. Bubble's visual interface speeds up these iterative changes, letting me adapt without diving too deep into code. I'll track progress monthly or quarterly, acknowledging which strategies yield the highest return and focusing my energy there for the next cycle.

REFLECTING ON THE BIG PICTURE

In the end, **SEO and marketing** in Bubble revolve around showcasing your app effectively on the web and guiding visitors toward meaningful actions—be it signing up, purchasing, or simply exploring. By polishing page titles, descriptions, and performance, you ensure search engines can easily surface your content. Then, with the help of analytics and integrations, you refine your marketing funnel based on real-world data, ensuring every campaign resonates with your audience.

What initially felt like a daunting aspect of building an online presence now sits at the heart of my success strategies. By combining Bubble's user-friendly development environment with a thoughtful SEO and marketing plan, I've found it possible to deliver a product that not only functions well but also steadily grows its user base. Once these foundations are in place, you can focus on scaling further, confident that new visitors know exactly what your app has to offer—and how to find it in the first place.

Chapter 24: Data Privacy and Regulatory Compliance

UNDERSTANDING THE IMPORTANCE OF PRIVACY

When I first realized I wanted to collect user information for my app—such as emails, billing details, or personal preferences—it dawned on me that this was more than just a technical challenge. I was stepping into the realm of data privacy and regulatory compliance. Bubble, thankfully, offers a host of tools to help you secure and responsibly manage user data, but it's ultimately on you to use them correctly. In this chapter, I want to walk through why these responsibilities matter and how to approach them in a Bubble context. Regardless of your industry or app size, respecting user privacy goes hand in hand with building trust and avoiding legal pitfalls.

DEFINING WHAT COUNTS AS PRIVATE DATA

Before diving into specifics, it's helpful to clarify which parts of your application might hold sensitive or private data. Often, it's anything that identifies or can be traced back to an individual: names, email addresses, phone numbers, credit card details, medical records, or geolocation. In Bubble, storing such details typically means creating data fields within the "User" data type or other custom data types. Understanding exactly which fields contain personal information is the first step toward building a compliance strategy. Once you know where that data lives, you can decide how to guard and limit access to it.

AN OVERVIEW OF COMMON REGULATIONS

Privacy rules vary depending on where your users reside and what your app does. However, there are a few key regulations that come up frequently:

- **GDPR (General Data Protection Regulation):** Covers individuals in the European Union (EU), focusing on the lawful processing of personal data and giving users certain rights (like the right to be forgotten).

- **CCPA (California Consumer Privacy Act):** Pertains to residents of California, demanding transparency about data collection and giving consumers control over their information.
- **HIPAA (Health Insurance Portability and Accountability Act):** A U.S. regulation for sensitive health data, applying to apps handling protected health information.
- **Other Local Laws:** Many regions or countries have their own rules, such as PIPEDA in Canada or PECR in the UK. Pay attention to user location to figure out what applies to you.

It can look daunting at first, but Bubble's privacy roles, data handling capabilities, and user consent tools go a long way in helping you respect these frameworks. The next sections detail practical ways to set up your app so you meet these obligations.

USING BUBBLE'S PRIVACY RULES EFFECTIVELY

Bubble's privacy tab is one of your main safeguards for controlling who can view or modify specific fields in your database. In my experience, carefully setting up these rules on each data type is the quickest way to ensure you aren't accidentally exposing personal information. Here's how I like to approach it:

1. **Identify Data Types That Contain Sensitive Info:** If "User" holds emails and payment data, you want strict rules on it. The same goes for health

records or user-generated content that might be private.
2. **Create Roles:** Define roles that distinguish between "Logged-in user," "User is this thing's creator," "Admin," or "Public/Everyone." Bubble allows you to set up multiple conditions so you can be as broad or narrow as necessary.
3. **Restrict Field Visibility:** For instance, let only the user themselves and possibly an admin see an email field. If you don't need that info to appear in a repeating group, hide it from non-owners altogether.
4. **Test Rigorously:** I always go through an incognito browser or a non-admin test account to confirm that off-limits fields remain hidden. This helps me catch any overlooked settings.

Conducting this privacy pass early on in development safeguards your app from the start. Any time you add new fields or data types, remember to revisit the privacy tab and update accordingly.

SECURING DATA IN TRANSIT AND AT REST

Bubble secures app data in transit via SSL (HTTPS), which is enabled by default on paid plans and is vital for protecting sensitive information from eavesdropping. For storing data at rest, Bubble relies on secure hosting with Amazon Web Services (AWS). While Bubble handles much of this behind the scenes, you still need to do your part:

- **Enable SSL on Custom Domains:** If you use a custom domain, confirm SSL is active. The lock icon in your browser bar demonstrates encryption is working.

- **Minimize Exposure:** Avoid sending personal data to third parties via unencrypted webhooks, or exposing it in query parameters. Bubble's API Connector and privacy rules let you manage data more discreetly.
- **Use Strong Password Policies:** Encourage complex user passwords or implement multi-factor authentication if your data is especially sensitive.

USER CONSENT AND TRANSPARENCY

Regulations like GDPR emphasize user consent and the right to know how their data is being handled. Bubble gives you multiple ways to practice transparency:

1. **Display a Privacy Policy:** Provide a link to a clearly written policy, either in the footer or as part of sign-up. Outline what data you collect, why, and with whom it's shared.
2. **Cookie Consent Banners:** If you use analytics or track user activity in a way that sets cookies, a small banner explaining cookie usage can help satisfy EU requirements.
3. **Opt-in for Marketing:** Separate sign-ups for mailing lists or promotional updates from account creation. That way, users actively consent to marketing emails instead of being automatically added.

When users understand what's happening with their data, they're likelier to trust your app. And from a compliance standpoint, you're in better shape by giving them control over these decisions.

HANDLING DATA DELETION AND USER REQUESTS

Another cornerstone of modern privacy laws is the user's ability to manage their data—whether that's seeing what you store or requesting its deletion. I typically plan for these scenarios by offering a few features:

- **Profile Management Page:** Let users edit or remove their personal details freely, encouraging a sense of control.
- **Account Deletion Option:** A user might want to fully remove their account. Build a workflow allowing them to request, confirm, and then delete the relevant record(s).
- **Export Features:** If you're dealing with data subject to GDPR, letting someone export their info can fulfill "Right to Access" requirements. You can generate a CSV or PDF summarizing their records.

I advise using backend workflows for some of these processes—like removing multiple related entries across your database. Just ensure you confirm the user's identity before enabling a full account purge, to prevent misuse.

HIPAA AND OTHER SPECIALIZED REQUIREMENTS

If your Bubble app handles health data, or other niche data categories, you might need additional safeguards beyond the default. HIPAA compliance, for example, mandates a

Business Associate Agreement (BAA) with hosting providers and strict audit trails showing who accessed patient info. While Bubble has a HIPAA-compliant plan in partnership with their hosting, you should carefully review the features included and see if they meet your medical application's needs. This typically involves more granular logs, carefully managing user permissions, and ensuring secure backups.

MAINTAINING AN AUDIT TRAIL

In certain regulatory environments, you'll need to demonstrate when data changes were made and by whom. Bubble doesn't automatically log every edit in a centralized audit table, but you can create your own system. For example, you might:

1. **Add Log Entries:** Each time a user updates a critical record, trigger a backend workflow to create a "log" entry containing who made the change, what changed, and when.
2. **Archive Sensitive Edits:** If you must keep version histories, store older record versions in a separate data type for reference (though be sure to apply privacy rules here as well).

This approach can be helpful not only for compliance but also for diagnosing issues that result from accidental or malicious edits.

STAYING CURRENT WITH EVOLVING LAWS

Data privacy regulations evolve quickly. New guidelines emerge, existing ones get updated, and user expectations keep rising. For peace of mind, I make it a habit to check relevant regulatory websites or consult legal professionals periodically. A handful of areas to watch include:

- **Changes in EU Data Transfers:** If you host in the U.S. but serve EU users, keep an eye on rules about data transfers across borders.
- **California Privacy Updates:** CCPA has expanded into CPRA, refining consumer rights further. Make sure you're up-to-date if you have a Californian audience.
- **Emerging Global Laws:** Countries like Brazil (LGPD) and Australia are updating their frameworks, which might affect how you handle users from those regions.

While Bubble can't solve every legal question, ensuring you know what's on the horizon helps tailor your app's structure or data flows before non-compliance risks grow.

FINAL THOUGHTS

Taking data privacy and regulatory compliance seriously is a hallmark of a professional, user-centric application. It not only builds confidence in your user community but also protects you from potential fines and reputational damage. Bubble's environment is already designed to make many aspects of data protection simpler—through privacy roles, built-in SSL, and flexible workflows—but it's how you use these features and structure your app that truly matters.

Whenever I embark on a new Bubble project that involves sensitive data, I map out the information flow and label each step with security measures. From verifying who can see or edit which fields, to offering export and deletion features, these practical steps ensure compliance is woven into the foundation of the app. Ultimately, being thorough and transparent about user privacy is one of the best ways to cultivate trust and loyalty in your growing community.

Chapter 25: Project Management and Collaboration

When I first started working on Bubble projects with other people, I noticed that effective collaboration wasn't just about dividing up tasks. It involved setting clear goals, choosing the right tools, and maintaining a smooth workflow so every contributor knew exactly what needed to be done. In this chapter, I want to share how I've approached planning, communication, and task management within Bubble—ensuring that projects move forward on schedule without anyone feeling lost.

DEFINING ROLES AND RESPONSIBILITIES

In my experience, the first step to good collaboration is clarifying who's responsible for which part of the app. Even if you're working with just one partner, it's helpful to detail areas of ownership. For instance, one person could focus on design and user interface, while another handles database structure or workflows. If you're collaborating with a larger group, you might assign distinct roles, such as:

- **Project Manager:** Oversees timelines, coordinates team communication, and tracks overall progress.
- **Designer:** Crafts the visual layout, color schemes, and user experience elements.
- **Workflow Specialist:** Focuses on logic, database interactions, and third-party integrations.
- **Tester:** Validates features, hunts for bugs, and confirms that updates don't break existing functionality.

Agreeing on these divisions from day one prevents confusion and avoids duplicated efforts as the project evolves. The Bubble Editor's access controls let you provide different permissions to each collaborator too. Depending on your plan, you can grant read-only access to testers or full edit permissions to core developers, maintaining tight control over your workspace.

USING TASK BOARDS AND MILESTONES

Even with an organized team, it's easy to lose track of smaller tasks. Early on, I adopted a task board (Trello, Asana, or any similar tool) to list features, bugs, and enhancements in separate columns. Each card outlines a task, the responsible person, and the due date. While this isn't exclusive to Bubble, linking your tasks to specific pages or user stories in the app can give everyone needed clarity.

For bigger goals—like delivering a working prototype or rolling out a beta—milestones are invaluable. I add these milestones to the board or calendar view so we have visible checkpoints. That way, it's obvious if a certain sub-feature is at risk of missing the broader deadline. Throughout the project, I'll reference these milestones in my Bubble Editor notes, reminding the team that the next "Beta Launch" or "UI Revamp" is coming soon.

COORDINATING EDITS IN REAL TIME

One of my favorite parts of working in Bubble is seeing updates happen live in the Editor—like two people simultaneously adjusting element properties or setting up workflows. If your plan supports multiple collaborators, Bubble shows who else is active, preventing overwrites and confusion. I do, however, encourage team members to communicate before making sweeping changes. For instance, if the Designer is about to reorganize the layout, a quick message in chat or a note in the task board helps others know to hold off on editing that same page.

I found that regular check-ins—either over voice calls or messaging apps—reduce the chance of stepping on each other's changes. We'd do short status updates where each person announces what they're working on and if they need help. This open communication plus Bubble's collaborative editing features gave us a synchronized workflow.

MAINTAINING ORGANIZED FOLDER STRUCTURES

As Bubble apps grow, the list of pages, reusable elements, and styles can get long. To keep everything manageable, I try to establish a naming convention early. For example, I'll name pages with a prefix like "admin_" or "public_" if that helps differentiate their function. Reusable elements might have "comp_" in front—short for component.

If you have a robust set of styles, I recommend grouping them by category (like "Buttons," "Text," "Inputs") and color-coding or labeling them in a uniform way. This prevents teammates from inadvertently creating near-duplicate styles. I also rely on the Elements Tree, especially if we have many nested groups on a single page. Giving each group a clear name—like "Group Header Nav" or "Group Main Content"—helps teammates recognize the structure at a glance, even if they aren't the one who built it.

REVIEWING CHANGES BEFORE MERGING

When multiple collaborators are active, it's wise to review changes in a testing environment before deploying them to the live version. Although continuous integration might not be as formal here as in traditional coding, I still treat the Bubble Development version like a staging ground. If someone finishes a new feature, they preview it and run basic tests to confirm it aligns with the task's acceptance criteria.

I'll often schedule a mini-review session once or twice a week where team members demo their updates. We'll gather feedback, log any adjustments in our task board, and only then make the decision to push those changes forward. This approach ensures that each piece of functionality passes at least one pair of fresh eyes—catching design inconsistencies or logical flaws early.

STAYING FOCUSED ON ITERATIVE IMPROVEMENTS

Early on, I fell into the trap of wanting the app to be perfect before letting anyone test it. Gradually, I shifted to a more iterative mindset: build a small slice of a feature, let teammates or beta users try it, collect feedback, and then refine. This shorter loop of development and feedback suits Bubble's no-code approach, as you can tweak and redeploy quickly.

Encouraging the team to think in terms of sprints or mini-releases also helps everyone keep momentum. Maybe one sprint focuses on user registration and onboarding, while another hones e-commerce checkout. This breakdown prevents the project from feeling overwhelming, as tasks become manageable chunks with clear definitions of done.

COMMUNICATING VIA COMMENTS AND NOTES

While external tools like Slack or email are great for broad discussions, I also discovered how helpful it is to leave notes directly in the Bubble Editor. For instance, I might add a text element in a hidden group that says, "Need to confirm final color palette," or place a comment in a workflow step telling other collaborators why I set a particular conditional.

These notes act like breadcrumbs for anyone who dives into the Editor after me. If they wonder, "Why does this pop-up hide automatically on page load?" they'll see my explanation, which can prevent accidental deletions or second-guessing. When the task is done or the design choice is approved, I remove or update these notes to keep the interface clean.

LEVERAGING INTEGRATIONS AND EXTERNAL SERVICES

If your project needs more advanced collaboration features—like time tracking or in-depth code reviews—you can connect Bubble to specialized services via APIs. For instance, if you want to measure the time each collaborator spends on design vs. workflow building, you could feed session data or updates into a project management platform. Similarly, if you have a complex pipeline for external code components (in custom plugins or scripts), you might store them in GitHub and reference them from inside Bubble.

Though Bubble won't replace every single tool a coder might use, the platform's flexibility in connecting with external resources ensures you can integrate your favorite project management, analytics, or design solutions as needed. That means your project can keep a consistent source of truth and process flows, even if your team uses multiple tools day to day.

RETROSPECTIVES AND CONTINUOUS REFINEMENT

No matter how smoothly a project runs, I've found it invaluable to pause at certain intervals—perhaps after each milestone—and hold a short retrospective. The question here is simple: "What went well, and what could we improve?" The team might realize they need more frequent check-ins, a better style guide, or deeper test coverage. Documenting these insights lets us refine our approach immediately. Then, each new phase of the project benefits from improved collaboration habits, leading to faster and cleaner outcomes.

FINAL THOUGHTS

Project management and collaboration in Bubble hinge on balancing a clear plan with the platform's flexible, real-time editing tools. By defining roles, using a reliable task management system, and communicating openly about progress, you set everyone up for success. When you fold short review cycles and iterative improvements into the mix, the entire development process remains adaptable, letting you pivot quickly whenever user feedback or fresh ideas   arise.

Personally, I've come to appreciate how Bubble's visual environment encourages conversation about design and logic. Instead of stats or lines of code, you're looking at real, interactive pieces your team can iterate on together. This naturally supports a more collaborative mindset, fostering an environment where each contributor can shine in their area of expertise, all while steering the project toward a shared goal.

Chapter 26: Testing and Quality Assurance

UNDERSTANDING THE VALUE OF RIGOROUS TESTING

One of the things I've learned from building web applications in Bubble is that the earlier you test, the smoother your final deployment tends to be. There's a sense of security that comes from knowing every workflow, page element, and piece of user data has been validated before going live. In my own projects, a thorough testing routine has saved me from launching features that sounded perfect in theory yet broke during real-world use. In this chapter, I want to share how I approach testing and quality assurance in Bubble—covering everything from basic functionality checks to stress testing and user feedback loops.

THE DIFFERENT FACETS OF BUBBLE TESTING

At first, "testing" just meant clicking through my pages to see if they did what I expected. Eventually, I realized how many layers are involved: verifying database structures, ensuring workflows respond correctly to edge cases, and validating design consistency across devices. Quality assurance in Bubble typically involves:

- **Unit Tests:** Checking individual workflows or small sets of elements in isolation.
- **Integration Tests:** Making sure interconnected features—like a sign-up form that triggers an email sequence—work together seamlessly.
- **User Experience (UX) Reviews:** Confirming pages look correct, remain responsive, and don't confuse new visitors.
- **Performance and Load Tests:** Determining how your app behaves under heavier user traffic or repeated data operations.

Combining these perspectives can uncover subtle bugs that a single round of clicking won't reveal, saving you time and user frustration in the long run.

USING DEBUG MODE AND LOGS

When I'm troubleshooting a particular workflow, I rely heavily on Bubble's debug mode. By appending "?debug_mode=true" to my preview URL, I can step through each action in the workflow and see which conditions evaluate to true or false. This level of granularity makes it easier to spot an issue—like a condition that references the wrong field or a missing data value.

Additionally, Bubble offers logs that record success and error messages from server-side actions (such as scheduled workflows). Reviewing these logs is my go-to method for verifying that each step executed as planned. If something isn't firing, there's a good chance the log will show me an error code or a blocked condition. By systematically checking the log entries after running a workflow, I can pinpoint exactly where and why a failure occurred.

SETTING UP A TEST ENVIRONMENT

Even though Bubble provides a visual editor and multiple versions, I still prefer to have a dedicated test or "sandbox" version. This is where I play with new features, load in sample data, and attempt all sorts of unusual use cases to uncover hidden breaks. Setting up a test environment is straightforward: I duplicate my main or development version and label it as "testing" or "staging." Then, I perform feature experiments there, safe from any risk of affecting my production environment.

Once I'm done, merging changes from the test environment back into development is a breeze. If I spot trouble during testing—like a conflict with existing workflows—I can revise and retest before reintroducing anything to the main build. This process keeps my core version stable and spares end users from half-finished ideas or frequent interruptions.

MANUAL VS. AUTOMATED CHECKING

Manual testing—clicking around, pretending to be a new user, or methodically checking forms—is a big part of my routine. However, once my app grows and I'm dealing with numerous workflows, manual checks can become tedious. In that situation, I might explore partial automation. For instance, by using external browser-based testing tools (like

Selenium or other services) that simulate user actions and verify the app's responses. Although Bubble doesn't natively integrate with test automation suites, you can often embed external tools or rely on no-code solutions that facilitate these checks.

Full-fledged automation requires some technical overhead and time investment, so I usually weigh the project size and frequency of updates. If I'm pushing daily updates or collaborating with a large team, automating at least some tests can save huge amounts of time. But for smaller apps, thorough, well-documented manual testing might suffice.

INVITING BETA USERS AND COLLECTING FEEDBACK

As valuable as internal testing is, nothing replaces real users putting your app through its paces. I often run a private beta phase where a small group tries out new features, logs in from various devices, and attempts tasks I might never have considered. In Bubble, it's easy to invite them to the development or a staging version, so they can poke around without risking the live product. Because every user's workflow is tracked, I can see error logs or usage patterns in Bubble's internal analytics or external trackers if integrated.

I funnel all beta feedback—be it bug reports or usability complaints—straight into a structured list. That might be a simple spreadsheet or a tool like Trello, where I can categorize issues as "critical," "minor," or "enhancement." This categorization helps me prioritize fixes. Especially in user-focused apps, a good chunk of insights can appear only once new eyes and fresh perspectives engage with the interface.

PERFORMANCE AND LOAD TESTING

Beyond ensuring everything functions, I also check how my app holds up under heavier loads. If I anticipate many people arriving at once—maybe after a big marketing push—I want confidence that the system won't grind to a halt. While Bubble autoscaling helps, it's still possible to bump up against capacity limits if workflows are complex or data queries are large.

One strategy I use is to run small-scale load simulations: I gather a handful of testers to simultaneously create accounts, submit forms, or generate new data. This live scenario often reveals bottlenecks (like an inefficient repeating group query) or points to workflows that cause minor slowdowns when triggered by multiple users at once. I might also consider a backend scheduling approach for tasks that can be deferred, reducing the real-time load on my front-end. If usage outstrips current capacity during these tests, upgrading or optimizing the logic can keep everything responsive when real traffic arrives.

BUILDING A COMPREHENSIVE QA CHECKLIST

Having a clear, repeatable QA checklist has saved me more times than I can count. Whether testing an MVP or finalizing major updates, I go through items like:

- **Login and Signup:** Does everything smoothly handle correct and incorrect credentials? Are error messages displayed appropriately?
- **Data Forms:** Are fields validated before saving? Do required fields block submission if left empty?
- **Workflows:** For each workflow, confirm that conditions trigger at the correct time and the final outcomes match expectations.
- **Responsive Layout:** Check how key pages behave on various screen sizes—desktop, tablet, mobile.
- **Edge Cases:** Attempt unusual inputs (like special characters, extreme numerical values) to see if the system gracefully handles them.
- **Access Controls:** Validate privacy roles, ensuring restricted data or admin pages are off-limits to regular users.

By turning these steps into a living document, I reduce the chance of forgetting to retest a feature touched by a recent update. Having a consistent checklist fosters confidence that each new rollout meets a minimum quality standard.

MAINTAINING MOMENTUM THROUGH ITERATIONS

In the final stretch, I remember that testing isn't a one-time event. Every new feature or bug fix can introduce new issues or break existing functionality. So I treat testing as an ongoing cycle: build, test, gather feedback, refine, and repeat. Each cycle might be short—maybe just an hour or a day, depending on the complexity—and then I push changes once things look stable. This iterative approach aligns with Bubble's visual nature, letting me deploy improvements fast without sacrificing thoroughness.

FINAL THOUGHTS

Testing and quality assurance in Bubble might look different from traditional coding environments, but the principles remain the same: verify early, test often, and welcome user feedback. By combining debug mode, thorough checklists, and real-world stress tests, you'll catch most issues before they ever reach the general public. The end result, in my experience, is a smoother launch, fewer frantic patches, and an app that earns users' trust through reliability. Whether you're a solo builder or part of a larger team, weaving QA into your development routine is one of the best ways to ensure your Bubble creation stands out for all the right reasons.

Chapter 27: Custom Plugins and Advanced Features

When I first dove into Bubble, I was amazed by how quickly I could build a functional web app without tapping into complex coding. Yet, as my projects evolved, I encountered moments where I needed unique capabilities or a deeper level of customization. That's when I discovered custom plugins—a gateway to advanced features that extend beyond Bubble's default toolbox. In this chapter, I'll walk through why creating your own plugins can be so powerful, what the plugin-building process looks like, and how you can unlock specialized functionality to push your app's boundaries.

WHY CREATE A CUSTOM PLUGIN?

One of the many reasons I became a fan of Bubble was the vibrant plugin ecosystem. But occasionally, I had use cases that weren't addressed by existing extensions. Maybe I wanted a custom integration with a niche service or a special design element that wasn't readily available. Building my own plugin offered me three big benefits:

- **Total Control:** I could craft precisely the API calls, data parsing, or visual elements my app needed—no more, no less.

- **Reusability:** Once I had my plugin, any future Bubble project could tap into it, avoiding duplicative setup in each new app.
- **Community Value:** If I chose, I could share my plugin in the Bubble marketplace, letting others benefit from my creation (and potentially monetizing it, if that's an interest).

Whenever I bump into a design or functionality gap, the first question I ask is whether a custom plugin would solve it more gracefully than a cumbersome workaround. If the answer is "yes," I dive in—knowing I'll end up with a solution that feels tailor-made for my app.

OVERVIEW OF THE PLUGIN EDITOR

Bubble's Plugin Editor might seem daunting at first if you haven't handled any code, but it's designed to be relatively intuitive. In short, a plugin can include:

- **Element:** A custom visual component you can place on pages.
- **Action:** A step you can add to workflows, letting you run specialized procedures or code.
- **API Connection:** A set of calls to external services, including authentication details and data structures.

From the Plugin Editor interface, you can define parameters and types, upload or write scripts in JavaScript, and arrange how your plugin interacts with Bubble's data. This does require some coding if you're building advanced elements, but for purely API-based plugins, you can often rely on

Bubble's visual input fields that ask for an endpoint URL, headers, and JSON keys—similar to the built-in API Connector.

CREATING A SIMPLE CUSTOM ELEMENT

My first foray into custom elements was building a specialized chart widget that Bubble didn't natively support. The steps to do something similar might look like this:

1. **Initialize Your Plugin:** In the Plugin Editor, create a new plugin and give it a name and description. Decide if it's private to you or eventually shareable.
2. **Add a New Element:** Define its properties—like width, height, or any dynamic data you want to pass in from your Bubble pages. A property could be "dataList," for instance, which a user can populate with a repeating group's data.
3. **Write Rendering Logic:** In the "Element Code" section, you can write JavaScript. This code runs when the element mounts on a page. You might include a chart library or custom drawing instructions to show data visually.
4. **Update Real-Time Changes:** If you expect the data to shift while the page is live, add an "update" function so your element redraws itself whenever the incoming data changes.
5. **Publish and Test:** Once saved, move to your Bubble app, install your plugin, and drag the new element onto a page. Provide any fields or expressions it needs, then preview to confirm it renders correctly.

The reward? A unique, interactive visual component that you can't achieve with Bubble's default elements—and it's all integrated seamlessly into your workflows and design.

ADVANCED ACTIONS IN WORKFLOWS

Sometimes, a plugin doesn't need to appear visually at all. Instead, you might want a custom workflow action. For example, let's say you need to encrypt or decrypt text using a particular cryptographic library. You can build a plugin action that accepts an input (the text to encrypt), runs JavaScript behind the scenes, and returns the encrypted output to your Bubble workflow. I've found this particularly handy in scenarios like:

- **Manipulating Data:** Converting a file format, hashing passwords, or compressing strings before saving them to the database.
- **Triggering External Services:** If you want a specific sequence of calls or transformations, a plugin action can handle them in code, then send results back into Bubble's next workflow step.
- **Running Complex Computations:** If Bubble's default expressions or built-in math functions don't suffice, you can use JavaScript to process arrays, filter objects, or do math operations. The plugin then feeds final values back to Bubble.

Building these advanced actions starts the same way: open the Plugin Editor, define a new "Action," specify inputs, write code, and specify outputs. Bubble automatically exposes that action in your app's workflow panel, letting you chain it among usual steps like "create a new thing" or "navigate to page."

CUSTOM API CONNECTIONS AND DATA TYPES

While Bubble's API Connector usually covers most external integrations, a custom plugin may be beneficial when you need to distribute or reuse a specific service across multiple apps. Suppose you're frequently using a particular payment processor or CRM that's not widely known. Creating a plugin to store all those endpoints and authentication logic means you only build them once. Here's how I handle it:

1. **Define the Auth Method:** If it's OAuth2, API Keys, or Bearer tokens, specify it within the plugin's "Add a new call" area.
2. **List Endpoints:** For each endpoint, specify the HTTP method, URL, and any parameters or headers. Use dynamic fields to let the plugin user fill in values from their own workflows.
3. **Set Return Data:** Provide a sample JSON response, so Bubble knows how to interpret each data field. This helps the user bind results to design elements or workflows seamlessly.
4. **Organize Fields:** If you plan to share the plugin on the marketplace, good documentation is crucial— label each input, note optional vs. required fields, and describe any quirks.

This approach fosters consistency. I no longer have to re-implement the same API calls or worry about copying credentials between apps. Everything I need is in one neat plugin.

DEBUGGING AND EVOLVING YOUR PLUGIN

Plugins often involve more trial and error than typical Bubble workflows, especially if JavaScript or external libraries are involved. I keep a few strategies in my back pocket:

- **Console Logging:** You can log debug messages in the plugin code, which appear in the browser's console. Perfect for checking if your data is arriving as expected.
- **Fallbacks:** If an API call fails or an action hits an error, bubble up a clear message to the app user or logs. This clarity speeds up troubleshooting.
- **Incremental Changes:** Start small—maybe define one element property or one endpoint—test thoroughly, then add more layers. Avoid building gigantic plugin logic all at once without debugging at each step.

And remember, as you refine your plugin, you can increment the plugin's version number. That way, if you break something inadvertently, you can roll back to a previous stable variant. Bubble manages these version states similarly to how it handles your main application's version control.

PACKING ADVANCED FEATURES INTO YOUR APP

Custom plugins are just one part of a broader "advanced features" realm. Over time, as your Bubble skills grow, you might experiment with items like:

- **Custom HTML/CSS:** Insert code blocks to refine your layout beyond standard Bubble constraints—like advanced animations or specialized grid systems.
- **Backend Data Transformations:** Combine scheduled workflows with plugin actions to handle large batch updates or real-time event triggers that rely on custom code.
- **Cross-App Integrations:** If you maintain multiple Bubble apps, let them communicate by creating a shared plugin that manages user data handoffs or unified analytics reporting.

These additions might move you closer to a "pro developer" experience—where you orchestrate multiple aspects of the platform—but they also unleash an incredible level of control and creativity that basic no-code approaches might never reach.

SHARING OR MONETIZING YOUR PLUGIN

Once your custom plugin is stable, you may choose to keep it private or publish it to the Bubble marketplace. I've done both, depending on the project. If I suspect the plugin solves a problem many Bubblers face, I'll make it public. Sometimes I'll even price it, turning a personal solution into a small revenue stream. If you do go public, consider these tips:

- **Documentation:** Write a short but thorough guide showing how to install, configure, and use every feature.
- **Clear Pricing (if any):** The marketplace supports one-time or subscription fees for premium plugins; ensure your listing clarifies what users get.
- **Version Updates:** Keep an eye on feedback from users, fix bugs, and roll out new releases. This fosters a positive reputation and can spur more downloads.

On the other hand, if your plugin is very niche or tied to a client's proprietary system, you might keep it private, accessible only to your own apps or those you specifically invite.

FINAL THOUGHTS

Venturing into custom plugins and advanced Bubble features transforms you from someone who merely assembles existing pieces into a creator who molds the platform to your exact vision. It might feel like a jump—especially if you're more comfortable in a purely no-code realm—but the payoff is huge. You'll tackle specialized integrations, create unique interface elements, and handle data in ways Bubble otherwise can't.

By experimenting step by step, you'll steadily build

confidence writing bits of JavaScript, configuring APIs, or refining design details that go beyond the standard constraints. The more you push these boundaries, the more your Bubble apps begin to stand out—not just as no-code prototypes but as fully customized, robust solutions that truly match your imagination.

Chapter 28: Monetization Strategies

When I first set out to monetize my work in Bubble, I realized that choosing the right strategy depended just as much on my audience's habits as on the app's functionality. Some users are comfortable with monthly fees, while others prefer one-time purchases or ad-supported models. The flexibility Bubble provides means you can blend different pricing approaches, experiment, and discover which structure resonates best with your audience. In this chapter, I'd like to walk through several popular monetization methods for Bubble apps—offering insights on how you can shape and test each one using the platform's built-in tools and integrations.

IDENTIFYING THE RIGHT REVENUE MODEL

My first step in monetization is always to ask: "What do users find most valuable here?" If your Bubble app helps people save time or manage projects efficiently, a recurring subscription might make sense. If you're showcasing premium content—like e-books, courses, or exclusive tools—you could consider a pay-per-download or paid membership approach. On the other hand, if you run a social platform with high user engagement, an ad-supported model or freemium tiers could be more effective. Above all, aligning your revenue model with the day-to-day benefits people get from your app is key to ensuring they feel good about paying.

SUBSCRIPTION AND MEMBERSHIP PLANS

A recurring subscription is one of the most prevalent monetization paths I've seen in Bubble apps. The platform's workflow logic and payment integrations allow you to handle monthly or annual billing without fuss. Typically, you'll define "Subscription Level" or "Role" fields on the user, then design workflows that trigger a payment when someone opts for a higher tier. Once payment completes, you automatically update their status, unlocking premium features like advanced searches, priority support, or extra data storage.

Taking it further, you can provide various membership tiers: "Basic," "Pro," "Enterprise," etc. Each tier can have distinct workflows for what's allowed—like the number of projects a user can create or the analytics they can view. In my own projects, I often add a "Check user's plan" condition to certain workflows, so if they haven't upgraded, the feature remains locked, and Bubble displays an upsell pop-up. This combination of visual cues and conditional workflows makes tier-based monetization remarkably straightforward.

FREEMIUM WITH PAID UPGRADES

Another popular model I enjoy testing is freemium: basic features remain open to all, while certain premium add-ons require payment. This balances attracting a wide user base—who use the free features daily—and converting a subset into paying customers for advanced functionality. With Bubble's conditional filters, you can easily show or hide these premium areas based on whether someone has purchased a specific product or unlocked an add-on in their account.

One example might be an analytics tool that offers free daily summaries but charges for in-depth, customizable reports. Users can experience the fundamental value of your app without committing money right away, building trust and familiarity before they consider upgrading.

ONE-TIME PURCHASES AND UPFRONT PRICING

If your app provides a distinct product—like a digital download, specialized document templates, or a unique plugin—charging a one-time fee can be more transparent for users. Instead of recurring payments, you set up a single workflow that processes the purchase and grants permanent access. This approach works especially well if you're distributing content people can reuse indefinitely or if your service is something they only need once (think event tickets or specialized research reports).

In my experience, keeping the buying process concise boosts conversions. I design a clean checkout page, tie it to a payment gateway, and finalize the sale in one or two steps. After purchase, either store a "purchase date" or "license key" in the user's record and refer to it in conditionals whenever they access that exclusive content, ensuring a frictionless path once they've paid.

ADVERTISING AND SPONSORSHIPS

For apps with a high volume of visitors or extended user sessions—like communities, content platforms, or social hubs—advertising can be a viable revenue generator. Bubble's plugin ecosystem supports embedding ads from networks such as Google AdSense. You can place these ads in sections of your layout where they don't disrupt the user's main   tasks.

Meanwhile, if your brand and user base are niche, sponsorships might prove even more lucrative. This could mean featuring a sponsor's banner, highlighting their product in a weekly newsletter, or integrating sponsored content in user feeds. I've found that clearly labeling sponsored sections while keeping the rest of the experience uncluttered is key to maintaining trust and not overwhelming the community.

MARKETPLACE OR TRANSACTION FEES

If your Bubble app facilitates transactions—like a job board, a local services marketplace, or a secondhand goods platform—you can capitalize by collecting a small fee per transaction. For example, if you run a marketplace linking sellers with buyers, you charge sellers a percentage each time a product or service is sold. Implementing this in Bubble usually involves hooking into a payment provider that splits or reroutes a portion of the payment to you as the platform   owner.

To illustrate: I once built a micro-gig marketplace in Bubble. When a gig was sold for $10, the app automatically forwarded $8 to the seller and $2 stayed with me. Bubble workflows handled the math, updated each user's earnings balance, and triggered a confirmation email. It's all about structuring your data so you know which transactions you're entitled to a portion of, then letting your payment logic do the rest.

USING CONDITIONAL UPSELLS AND PROMPTS

A detail I find often overlooked is how you present upgrades or invitations to pay. Bubble's visual logic makes it easy to create a dynamic experience—for instance, showing an upsell banner only when a user attempts to access a premium feature for the second or third time. The message might read, "Enjoy unlimited usage by upgrading your plan," along with a seamless button to proceed to checkout.

You can also track usage in custom fields—like "reports_generated" or "projects_created"—and once the user hits a limit, display a pop-up that encourages them to remove the cap with a paid tier. By tailoring these messages contextually, you avoid bombarding users too soon, yet provide clear value statements when it matters.

FACILITATING SMOOTH PAYMENT FLOWS

Regardless of the monetization model, a frictionless payment experience is crucial. If your checkout or subscription process is convoluted, users may abandon their carts. I always keep my payment pages minimal: essential fields only, a concise summary of what they're buying, and prominent buttons to confirm or cancel. Let Bubble handle any email confirmations or invoices once the transaction completes—say, by scheduling a workflow that sends a receipt or updates the user's profile to "Paid."

To bolster trust, I often embed or reference secure payment logos or short disclaimers about data handling. If integration with a recognized payment gateway—Stripe, PayPal, or others—fits well, I add those badges to reassure paying users. Building that sense of security cuts down on hesitation and buyer friction.

EXPERIMENTING WITH PRICING AND OFFERS

No matter how confident I feel about a product's price, I find it vital to test multiple price points or promotional strategies. With Bubble, you can easily set up discount codes or time-limited deals: for example, a new user gets a first-month discount, or existing subscribers can refer a friend for a reduced rate. In the app's database, store a "promo code" record linking the discount amount to an expiration date. Then, at checkout, let the user input a code, and if valid, apply that discount to the transaction.

Each experiment—free trials, holiday sales, referral bonuses—provides data on user behavior. I typically measure conversion rates, average revenue per user, and subscription retention. Over time, noticing patterns in these metrics helps me refine how, when, and at what price I offer upgrades or sales, ensuring healthy revenue growth without alienating potential customers.

CONTINUOUS MONITORING AND REFINEMENT

Monetization isn't a static decision—it's an ongoing process. Monitoring user feedback, churn rates, and transaction data is essential for fine-tuning pricing, removing underused premium features, or adding new paid functionalities. Bubble's logs and integrated analytics (or external trackers) let you track how active paying users are, whether they remain subscribed after the first billing cycle, and which features drive the most engagement.

I usually set a monthly or quarterly checkpoint to revisit my monetization model in light of these metrics. Maybe a feature I thought should be premium belongs in the free tier to boost overall adoption, or maybe certain advanced tools that used to be free are valuable enough to be paywalled. By keeping an open mind, I ensure my app's evolution reflects user feedback and the actual revenue patterns rather than initial assumptions.

FINAL THOUGHTS

Monetization on Bubble can be as flexible as the platform itself. Whether you opt for subscriptions, one-time payments, in-app ads, transaction fees, or sponsored placements, Bubble's design and workflow tools help you translate these strategies into a seamless user experience. My advice is to pick an approach that's consistent with your app's core value proposition, implement it carefully, and then experiment with variations. Over time, you'll find that sweet spot where your revenue model benefits both you and your community—ensuring that the efforts you've poured into building a great Bubble application pay off in a sustainable, rewarding way.

Chapter 29: Case Studies and Real-World Examples

When I first began building apps in Bubble, I found myself wondering what it really looked like in the wild—how others were using the platform for real business goals, side projects, or community-driven tools. Over time, I've gotten to see firsthand just how far a determined Bubble creator can go. In this chapter, I want to share a handful of real-world examples that spotlight the variety of projects you can build and scale without writing traditional code. My hope is that these stories inspire you to envision fresh possibilities and confidently tackle your own Bubble ambitions.

TURNING A HOBBY MARKETPLACE INTO A BUSINESS

An acquaintance of mine had a passion for collecting handmade crafts. She realized there was a niche of artisans who needed a place to sell specialty items, but didn't want the complexity or fees of larger platforms. So she decided to create a small marketplace with Bubble—one that would connect crafters to interested buyers in a more personal and curated way.

The most impressive part was how quickly she spun up essential features: user sign-up, product listings, a shopping cart, and a checkout flow integrated with payment gateways. She set up basic search filters so buyers could find items by category or price range, and added a ratings system to highlight top sellers. By leveraging Bubble's built-in database and repeating groups, she was able to handle dozens of craft listings in no time. When interest grew, she upgraded to a paid plan to get more capacity and implement real-time chat support between creators and customers.

Today, her marketplace brings together hundreds of artisan sellers and fans. Frequent updates—like limited-time promotions and an event calendar—happen seamlessly through Bubble's visual editor. This case study showed me how someone with vision and passion can stand up a functional, revenue-generating web app without outsourcing heavy development work.

AUTOMATING INTERNAL PROCESSES FOR A SMALL COMPANY

Another scenario I found inspiring was a small logistics firm that managed deliveries for local merchants. Before Bubble, they used spreadsheets and piles of emails to coordinate pickup times, route drivers, and confirm drop-offs.

Needless to say, errors piled up, and employees spent too much time sending repetitive messages.

Using Bubble, the company's office manager built a centralized portal. Drivers had their own login, which displayed daily tasks, real-time maps, and status buttons to mark a delivery in progress or completed. Managers could see an overview of all scheduled deliveries, filter them by driver or urgency, and track metrics like average delivery time.

The payoff was immense: fewer mistakes, faster dispatching, and automated notifications that saved hours of back-and-forth communication. Their solution wasn't flashy, but it made operations flow more efficiently. Adopting Bubble gave them an internal system they could tweak any time changes were needed, whether that meant rearranging data fields or adding an extra step for special requests. This emphasized how Bubble isn't just for public-facing apps—it can transform behind-the-scenes processes too.

LAUNCHING A PERSONALIZED COURSE PLATFORM

A friend of mine, a professional coach, dreamed of hosting online workshops and interactive quizzes tailored to each student's progress. She had tried a few learning management systems, but they didn't offer the personalization or branding she wanted. Finally, she turned to Bubble to create her own platform.

Her app allowed students to enroll in courses, each with modular lessons that unlock only once the previous lesson's quiz is passed. She embedded text, videos, and animation using Bubble's responsive design engine, ensuring the layout stayed polished on phones or laptops. On the back end, she generated progress reports that showed each student's completion rate and quiz scores. If someone needed extra guidance, she could schedule one-on-one sessions directly in the platform.

All of these features tied together seamlessly with user roles, email reminders, and dynamic pages for each student's dashboard. Over time, as she gathered more feedback, she added features like discussion forums and group projects—again, iterating without rewriting massive chunks of code. This success illustrated how, by combining Bubble's no-code workflows with a structured content flow, you can build an engaging course platform from the ground up in record time.

RAPID MVP FOR STARTUP VALIDATION

I've also met entrepreneurs who rely on Bubble for their minimum viable products (MVPs). One founder told me how critical it was to prove his idea—a peer-to-peer ride-sharing concept—before pitching investors. Instead of spending months (and a significant budget) on a custom-coded app, he set up a Bubble MVP in just a few weeks, with core functions like requesting a ride, a driver-accept flow, and a location-based matching system.

Even though the location tracking element required integrations with third-party map and geolocation APIs, Bubble's plugin ecosystem simplified that process. He built a sign-up and login system, user profiles for riders and drivers, plus a basic rating mechanism once a trip was complete. Then, to test real-world feasibility, he launched in a small city, observed user behavior, and gathered feedback. Although the concept evolved into something else eventually, the MVP had given him enough actionable data to pivot early—saving considerable development costs and time. This underscores how a fast, functional prototype in Bubble can de-risk new ventures significantly.

COMMUNITY FORUM WITH REAL-TIME ENGAGEMENT

A small non-profit I volunteered with hoped to establish a private forum where members and volunteers could share stories, resources, and event updates. They wanted something more dynamic than typical email chains, but less complicated than mainstream social networks. In Bubble, they built a community page featuring topic threads, user mentions, and pinned announcements.

Custom states and repetitive groups made it possible to create a real-time feed of posts. Members could attach images or documents, upvote helpful replies, and tag staff if they needed official input. The non-profit also embedded an "events calendar" element that synced with each member's profile, sending out reminders for volunteer meetups.

With Bubble's robust privacy rules, they restricted content to only those invited, ensuring a safe space for discussions. Over time, the administrators expanded the forum with features like mentor matching and a resource directory—demonstrating how Bubble's modular design supports continuous community growth without needing to migrate or rebuild somewhere else.

LESSONS LEARNED FROM REAL PROJECTS

Across these case studies, a few themes consistently stand out:

- **Iterate Rapidly:** Each example highlights how quick iteration helps shape an app's direction. You can adjust logic, refine layouts, or add new pages without waiting on developers or writing raw code.
- **Focus on the Core Value:** Whether it's matching artisans to buyers or tutoring students, each builder started with a specific goal, used Bubble to implement critical features, and then expanded gradually.
- **Use Existing Integrations:** Payment gateways, map systems, or analytics tools are readily available in the Bubble ecosystem. Lean on them when you need specialized functionality—there's no reason to reinvent the wheel.
- **Build for Scale:** While some projects remain small, others ramp up, requiring plan upgrades or more advanced workflows. Bubble's capacity-based approach and flexible data structures let founders scale without re-platforming.

INSPIRING YOUR OWN REAL-WORLD JOURNEY

The best part about seeing these real-world projects is realizing just how much is possible when you bring creativity and determination to Bubble. If you're at the idea stage, treat these examples as motivation. If you've already been prototyping, let them reassure you that you're on a solid path—one shared by marketplace founders, non-profit organizers, course creators, and more.

So whether your vision is a niche community, a new e-commerce store, a job board, or a communication hub for your team, the platform empowers you to dream big and iterate fast. You don't need a development army to craft apps that meet professional standards or market demands. As these stories prove, valuable, functioning products can spring to life at an impressive pace.

With a willingness to experiment and refine, who knows how far you might push your own Bubble creation? Perhaps you'll create the next marketplace success story, an internal app that dramatically changes how a small business operates, or a membership platform that fosters an entire community. In any case, these real-world results show that Bubble isn't just for demos or prototypes—it's truly a catalyst for bringing complete and thriving web apps into reality.

www.ingramcontent.com/pod-product-compliance
Lightning Source LLC
La Vergne TN
LVHW051227050326
832903LV00028B/2269

* 9 7 9 8 3 1 5 9 0 6 6 9 8 *